EIGHT DECADES
(and more)

Oliver R. Bishop

authorHOUSE®

AuthorHouse™
1663 Liberty Drive
Bloomington, IN 47403
www.authorhouse.com
Phone: 1-800-839-8640

Published by AuthorHouse 10/26/2012

ISBN: 978-1-4772-5723-4 (e)
ISBN: 978-1-4772-5724-1 (hc)
ISBN: 978-1-4772-5725-8 (sc)

Library of Congress Control Number: 2012914249

Any people depicted in stock imagery provided by Thinkstock are models, and such images are being used for illustrative purposes only.
Certain stock imagery © Thinkstock.

This book is printed on acid-free paper.

TABLE OF CONTENTS

FORWARD

No, these first few paragraphs are **not** entitled foreword. It is the discussion I had with myself about whether or not I should proceed with writing an autobiography. I didn't feel that I wanted to embark on some treatise for recognition or aggrandizement, and I certainly did not consider it to be an expanded resume. I had gained about all that I ever would in this game. I'm not good at blowing my own horn anyway. I'm not musician enough to add all the grace notes needed to pretty up an atonal composition.

When one first puts pen to paper, one must decide why he's doing it. I suppose, for my part, I would be doing it more as an attempt to inform, to entertain, and to somewhat serve as a genealogical footnote to those who may wish to climb this particular family tree. I did not want it to be some ego trip wherein my "great deeds" would be posted for posterity. No one wants to hear how great you are. If you're that good, it will all be in your obituary.

I knew the narrative should be readable by more than just the writer, or else, what's the point? I would be wasting my time, unless I was trying to expiate some dark sin. I also felt that the document should be as grammatically correct as possible. Otherwise, I would be displaying my own ignorance as well as the failure of the education system.

I knew that there would be considerable time and effort involved. Then I thought about how much fun it might be to look back and dredge up old memories--some good, some bad. Revisiting the past is okay if you have no apologies to make, except for a few embarrassing moments.

From my arguments with myself in the decision process about the project, I decided that the pluses outweighed the minuses, and I decided I would be forward enough to go forward ...

FOREWORD

This narrative is neither a diary nor a journal to which I have faithfully committed my innermost thoughts and desires. Nor is it an autobiography in which I attempt to relate all of my peccadilloes and my valiant accomplishments. It is hardly a book in the true sense of the word. It has no plot, no climax, nor a denouement. It is not historical or diachronic, since it has no impact upon any study of the past. It is simply a rambling, non-selective, quasi-chronological, chain of events strung together like ladyfinger firecrackers, some with longer fuses than others, and some of which, like the occasional firework, fizzle or do not go off at all.

I decided early on that the approaches, "I was born at a very early age," or "I was born in El Dorado, Kansas so I could be near my mother," had been overdone. Though there will be some tongue in cheek material, most of this will be pretty straight forward.

I offer no acknowledgments, no kudos for assistance along the way, no appreciation to others for things which may have been provided. I offer only a simple thanks to Mother and Dad for the germplasm, the genes, and the guidance that made me what I am.

In searching for ways to separate the various stages of life into years or maturation levels, my decision to liken the first part of my story to stages of a NASA flight was probably ill advised, and a bit too clever. After all, the later years may have had to contain chapters such as "Abort" and "Crash and Burn." That would have been a bit too grim, so I returned to more or less chronological headings. There are some little vignettes strewn about. I hope they do not affect the flow of the story.

I begin this "narrative about the activities and events of a given time" at its meager beginning, with how the "person who took part in them" came to be. Therefore, Part I, "A Life is Launched," reflects my own as well as the narrative's beginning. In Part II, "Military Life: The Early Years," I move out into the world and start my years in the service, which takes up nearly a third of my life. Part III, "Military Life: The Middle Years," is an attempt to separate out my becoming an officer, and the subsequent years, from my enlisted career. In Part IV, "Twin Threads," another character or two is added to the narrative. I no longer am one person moving through the activities and events of my own life, but these events now involve a wife and family.

Part V, "The Cold Cruel World," covers the activities, and the many trials and tribulations met in the beginning of a new career, away from the protective bosom of the military. Part VI, "Retirement," is supposed to reflect all of the joyous events and good times that all of the years of hard work and planning have been preparing me for.

And so to Part I ...

O. R. B.
2012

PART I:
A LIFE IS LAUNCHED

I HAVE ALWAYS been a lover of science fiction and it was to this kind of literature that I gravitated during my formative years. I would walk, ride my horse and, even sleep, it seemed, with an SF book in my hands.

I have chosen the above title for this part of the narrative and subsequent chapters therein, from those steps which relate to putting a missile in space. However, at the time of my own small launching, there was no glimmer of the kind of travel which one could achieve earth or lunar orbit, except perhaps, in the mind and the stories of Jules Verne and other noted science fiction writers.

The launching of a life, as with the launching of a space vehicle, is a very complicated process. In both, there are many millions of components, any one of which can go wrong at the worst possible time. With a human life the number of components outnumber those of a space vehicle, but one does not give that much consideration.

There is seldom as much thought given to the launching of a life as there is with the launching of a space vehicle. If there was, there would be fewer of us around. The initial procedures are not as complicated with a life, but no mission control officer ever had to hang around for years and years after the launch to determine whether his mission was going to be successful or not. Nor did he ever have to sit up all night wondering if his charge simply had a bad cold or was it something more serious.

With raw materials refined, designs carefully engineered, products manufactured, components assembled, and orbits plotted, it is now time to launch, so we move to Chapter One: "Countdown."

CHAPTER ONE:
COUNTDOWN

AS WITH ALL countdowns there is a confirmation that all logistics problems have been satisfied, which includes everything from paperwork to fuel. The countdown must compare all related data for anomalies. The mission will abort if all requirements are not in place. In this instance there was an assembling of the gene pool to properly configure the missile.

Logistics Assembled

The logistics of getting a payload of eight pounds, eight ounces into orbit requires much early preparation. The Bishop component of the payload originated in Scotland and Ireland, and came to America during the potato famine in Ireland. The Bishops first settled in Illinois, they later moved to Missouri where my father, Oliver Harrison, was born. They then moved to Oklahoma, to try to scratch out a living from the red soil around the "East Bend of the South Canadian River." Their original intention in going to Oklahoma was to participate in the land rush of the "Oklahoma Strip" run, but they arrived too late. They later moved to Kansas in 1907. The inside joke of later years was that Father and Mother came to Kansas the same year. 1907 is the year that Mother was born.

The Gharsts, my father's mother's family, were first generation German and were farming in the small community of Potwin, east of El Dorado, Kansas. It was here that my grandfather met and married the oldest daughter, Sarah. Several genealogical searches of that branch of the family have proven that there are still a lot of Gharsts out there.

My mother's father, Oscar Garabrandt, had come from Ohio as an orphan and married into the land-rich Rodwell family. It was long suspected that Oscar may have been an orphan or an "Orphan Train" child, which was simply an unwanted child of a poor family sent West on a train from New York or another large city to be adopted by a family in need of an extra pair of hands to help farm the land. My grandfather arrived in Kansas with little more than the clothes on his back. He was just old enough to leave his adoptive family and strike out on his own.

He was always very close-mouthed about his past, and many attempts to trace his name and background through genealogical records have been unsuccessful. One source shows that he was little more than an unpaid employee of his adoptive family.

The Rodwells, my maternal grandmother's family, were a part of the landed gentry in England and had made their way to America to buy land. They first went to Wisconsin, then to California, where Jonathan Rodwell left the family to hunt for gold. The rest of the family came to Kansas and purchased a large farm.

That family was headed by the matriarch, Sarah Rodwell. The husband never returned to the home. There were many fanciful tales that he had been murdered for his gold mine. Letters came from a person who had supposedly buried him, and attested to the fact that Jonathan had struck it rich. The children prospered, however, and the first son, David, married a Graham. Juliette (Graham) Rodwell died in childbirth. Sarah raised the daughter, Daisy Bell, who was to become my grandmother.

Daisy had an early childhood accident falling from a ladder. Her back was injured and became severely misshapen as she grew older. It was to her that Oscar Garabrandt was married. The marriage was probably an arrangement--a penniless Dutchman, to a daughter who was no catch physically, but potentially land rich. They each got something from the deal. Among the things that they obtained were three children: Hazel May, Kenneth, and Helen Elizabeth. Hazel, my mother, was the first born.

When poking about in the dusty archives of my family history, I had hoped to find some villains or heroes that would make my search worthwhile. The closest to some interesting stuff that I found was my great-grandfather was murdered for his gold mine, my father's father supplying "firewater" to the Indians in Oklahoma for cash, and his allegedly having given one of the James gang a ride, for which he was awarded a $5.00 gold piece, which was big money to him.

There was a drummer boy, Samuel Pickerill, Jr., a third great grandfather who was in the Revolutionary War, thus, authorizing my daughters to be members of the DAR. That honor, however, seems not to be as treasured as it once was.

Telemetry Established

My father was a day laborer with a threshing crew when he first saw my mother. She was bringing water to the men in the fields. Father allegedly made the remark to his buddies that he was going to marry that girl. Their next encounter was on a country road. Mother was returning home from school with school-mates. She was in the eighth grade. Father was driving a team and wagon with a load of hay. He bantered with her, calling her cute names, and did little more than embarrass her.

About a week later he arrived at my grandmother's house at milking time. He introduced himself to Grandmother, helped finish the milking, and then asked if he could come calling on her daughter. My grandmother was a bit concerned about the age difference, but my father could be very charming when he had to be.

It didn't take too many trips to the movies before talk of marriage became serious. Mother had graduated from the eighth grade, but there were no prospects of high school, and she did not wish to spend any more time at home working as a hired hand without any compensation. To avoid all of the talk they drove to Eureka, the County seat of the next County, and were married on December 18, 1923. Mother was sixteen and Father was thirty-one.

Minus 10 (9 months??) and Counting

Mother and Father put off having children for two reasons. The first was simply to prove beyond the shadow of a doubt that the marriage was not a "shotgun" wedding, and the second was that Mother did not want children so young. Perhaps another reason was that they were not very well off financially. Father continued to be a day laborer and they were living part of the time with Father's parents.

In fact, Father continued to be somewhat of a gypsy during his entire life. He was always ready to move "at the drop of a hat." Mother always had the deep seated feeling of wanting roots and permanence. She would always cry when Father would announce another move. I suppose I inherited my desire for a stable home life from my mother.

In the normal course of events, Mother became pregnant. The pregnancy was normal, but my size caused some very traumatic birthing problems involving forceps and a complicated labor. At last I arrived, eight pounds, eight ounces, at 4:45 p.m., Wednesday, December 5, 1928.

Henry Ford introduced his Model A Ford in 1928. Oliver and Hazel Bishop introduced Richard, an entirely different model--countdown complete.

It might be appropriate here to indicate who "Richard" is. I was named Oliver after my father, with Richard as my middle name, because mother liked the name. Though my first name is Oliver, I was never called that at home, nor was I called Junior. I was never "Ollie", nor "Dick" at home. Mother abhorred that diminutive of Richard. Actually, to my parents I was Sonny, or Sonny Richard, until I left home.

At school I was Richard, which caused a minimum of confusion, but when I entered the work-a-day world it became Dick. In the military it was Bishop. Back again to civilian life, I gave up trying to explain my name and became Oliver for the first time. Dad would have been proud.

Mother and Father

Perhaps here would be a good place to introduce my parents as the couple they were, rather than genealogically.

Their marriage was loving and stable. It was no hearts and flowers kind of life for them. There were few times that I saw them demonstrably affectionate. Their marriage was simply an enduring, quiet, caring.

Their lives were simple. They could not afford to dream. Their dreams were wrapped in the future accomplishments of their children. Those accomplishments did not necessitate climbing mountains, being President, or curing cancer. They wanted the simple things for their children: a good marriage, healthy happy grandchildren, with food for them to eat, and a roof over their heads. I can see them now, Dad in his overalls (patches on top of patches), a faded flannel shirt and a hat, always a hat. And Mom in a faded house dress with an apron atop it, always the apron. Most often there was a dishtowel in her hand. Dad always had a claw hammer and a pair of pliers at hand. He was of the opinion that if it couldn't be fixed with those tools, it wasn't worth having.

In our family there was always all that fixing, patching, repairing, and reusing. It was a way of life that sometimes made me crazy. I wanted just once to be wasteful. Waste meant you could afford something new. Throwing things away meant you could buy more. But at home, in our family, you salvaged, reused, patched, and "made do" with things that were never quite right for the job.

My parents' friends and family usually lived a long drive away. It took preparation to visit them. They had to get up early to get all the chores done--milking, livestock feeding, etc. This was to give them time enough time to visit before they had to start back home to take care of those eternal chores--milking, feeding, watering, gathering eggs, etc.

When Dad finally was too frail to be far from a doctor and his eyesight too poor to let him drive his old truck, I bought a house for them and moved them to the city. There was indoor plumbing, running water, and natural gas for heat and cooking. No more carrying water or chopping wood to keep them from freezing.

Dad never took to city living. He gave up being productive. He wore out several decks of cards playing solitaire, but he no longer took much interest in anything. When Dad passed at age 78 he set a genetic mark to follow. Any male heir living past 78 is living on borrowed time. At past 80, at this writing, I can only hope that my mother's age of 93 at her passing will counter that a bit.

Mother loved the city. Friends and relatives were close, and for a while she could drive to the stores and to see her friends. After a few auto accidents, the driving was no longer possible, but she never lost her sense of *joie de vivre*.

Toward the end when cancer was infecting her, Mother still seemed to hang on to a youthful spirit. It was when she died that my sisters and I came to the stark realization that we were truly orphans now, with no one left to really "come home to."

I think that I finally came to the final painful realization things are not forever. They get used up, wear out, go away, never to return. I had the very first introduction to that when I was three and I broke my favorite toy.

So, while we have something we love, it is best that we take care of it and try to fix it when it's broken, or try to heal it when it's ill. This is true for friends, marriages, favorite toys, old cars, and aging parents. We try to keep them because they are worth it. They are links to our past

Some things you can keep, like pictures, old love letters, and keepsakes collected from your travels. They are small objects that link us to the past and happier times and to the things that seem to make life important, like family and old friends.

CHAPTER TWO:
I HAVE COGNITION

WHILE THE TITLE of this chapter is a play on the words: "We have ignition," there is considerable parallel here. The rocket engines start with the igniting of the fuel. Cognition is the firing of neurons in the brain, and the sparking at the synaptic junctions which bring about memory. I am yet reminded of René Descartes' statement, "*Cogito, ergo sum*" (I think, therefore I am). I guess I am (do exist), because I started thinking (and remembering) pretty early.

First Memories

The first remembered sensory impulses after my synapses were functioning were not preceded by any flashes of light, color, sounds or smells. My first glimmer of memory was implanted while I was in a space vehicle of sorts. I was suspended in space anyway. I recall that I was bouncing in one of those canvas baby seats, hanging in the middle of a doorway. My recollections were (and are) of the taste and texture of the canvas-covered bar at chin height in front of me. I must have been teething, because I recall chewing on the bar and a circular ring as well. I later learned that this ring was a celluloid harness ring.

My vision seemed limited in dimension. I could see a shiny linoleum floor and legs going back and forth, but I couldn't see, or at least focus, on anything much above my eye level. Once in a while those legs would come toward me and a larger shape would come down to my level. Sometimes this visit would result in the ring being put back in my hand, sometimes it meant that I was being lifted up. I don't remember for what purpose. I guess the altitude shut off that first memory tape.

The next memory, a bit more hazy than the first, was of me crawling about the brightly colored linoleum floor on my hands and knees. There was very distinctive music being played. Years later, when I would play our old Victrola, there were certain records that would cause me to relive that specific time when I was playing on the floor. I could still visualize my mother bustling about with her chores, stopping every once in a while to wind up the record machine.

In later years, my mother would be incredulous when I told her that I had retained those memories, since I was less than eighteen months old for both of them. I certainly didn't read about them, and they were simply too mundane to be repeated in a conversation so that I could have received the experience vicariously. There were other small vignettes of memory, but none so early and none so strong.

The Dog Bite

One early experience, which should have made an indelible impression, I do not remember in the least. My father had a female German Shepherd, which had just given birth to puppies. I was only a toddler, but had made my way to the place where the puppies were. Their mother did not like my attention, so she took a large bite out of the left side of my face. The bite did not puncture my eye, but tore it out of its socket and ripped my cheek open. A family doctor put my eye back in and sewed everything back together. He allegedly remarked on how lucky I had been not to have lost my eye. I carried the scars in my eyebrow and on my cheek for over twenty years after this event.

I suppose that this incident was just too traumatic for my brain to comprehend, because I remember things both before and after the dog bite. My father was devastated by the incident. Even though I should have been minding my own business, and the dog was only protecting her puppies, my father was so angry that he destroyed both the bitch and her puppies. My mother, who related the story to me in detail several times in later years, was sorry that I had been bitten, but was totally dismayed at the retaliatory actions of my father.

I would not wish to be echoing any psycho-babble regarding the effects of the dog bite, but during my entire life I never did care very much for dogs. Nor did I truly have any pets when I was a child. We always had dogs, cats, and any number of barnyard animals on the farm, and later on the ranch. However, there was never any that I recall having thought of as mine alone, or one that I cared for over all others.

I supposed the closest I came to having a pet of my own was for a short period of time when I had a bantam rooster called Corky. He slept in the house on the back of a chair, with a newspaper spread strategically under him. With his first crowing in the morning, he was thrust outside to fend for himself until evening, when he would come to the door at the time all other chickens made their way to the chicken house. I don't recall what caused his demise, but I remember my mother helping me scratch his name on a shingle which served as his headstone when we buried him.

White Horse

I always liked the soft, furry animals: baby chickens, and ducklings, kittens and puppies. However, I never made any attachments, because they too soon were no longer soft and cuddly. From the time of my earliest memories until well into my grammar school years, my friend and companion was an imaginary one. It was a white horse. I did not have a pet name for it. I simply called it "White Horse." I cannot now say whether it was male or female, however, in retrospect, I guess it was male.

I seldom rode White Horse. I generally ran with him or lay down with him as if he were a security blanket. When I really needed more security, I would go inside of him and be protected. I do not know how *that* process worked. I just know that I was able to get inside him where I felt safe and secure.

I don't know where I got the idea for this beautiful white horse as my imaginary companion. We only had big draft horses on the farm at this time. I do know that my parents were fans of Western movies. I may have picked up "White Horse" from one movie image, or a composite of many, without knowing it. This was certainly before the popularization of *The Lone Ranger*, with his white horse "Silver."

Grandmother's House

One image that comes to mind was my grandmother poking at me with a stick, trying to dislodge me from under her bed. It was much later that I learned that I had been placed in my maternal grandmother's care while my mother was in the hospital for the birth of my brother. I was only three at the time. I wanted to get away from everyone and could not understand why my mother was not around. My grandmother gave up in disgust with my actions and decided that I would come out when I got hungry. When I finally decided that White Horse would not solve this problem, I crawled out after an hour or two under the bed.

I can remember that event with my grandmother and some other minor activities around my grandparent's house on that occasion, but I cannot remember my mother and father coming to get me to take me home. They did not bring me a baby brother, and the sadness of that event probably did much to make the situation non-memorable. My mother was to have named him William Henry after my fraternal grandfather. He was born September 20, 1932. There was seldom any talk about his having died in childbirth. It was not until Mother was in her sixties that she began to make regular visits to his grave.

While here at Grandma's, let me tell one other memory. During this period, my parents did not live too far from my grandmother. It seemed that every Sunday we drove to her house for Sunday dinner. I guess it was sort of like charity on Grandma's part. Anyway, the fare was always the same ... fried chicken.

Grandma's yard was always full of chickens. There were always chickens everywhere. She would simply go out, sneak up on a young rooster and wring its neck right there. I didn't want to watch, but I would stare fascinated as the headless rooster would flop and flop for the longest time, spraying his blood from his neck. After that gruesome sight I could still polish off a drumstick. Go figure.

My First Christmas

Not really my first Christmas, but the first one I remembered. This occurred when I had just turned three. We had a tradition in the family that Santa Claus arrived on Christmas Eve. Presents could be found and opened any time on Christmas Eve. I recall that my mother had baked a cake and was frosting it with boiled icing, which required whipping egg whites into hot sugar syrup. While Mother was beating the egg whites, my father asked me if I wanted to gather eggs with him. This evening chore of gathering eggs was usually done with my mother, so it was a great treat to accompany my dad to the hen house for this task. I was somewhat amused that Dad seemed to be taking an unusually long time to gather the few eggs that were in the nests. I merely assumed that it was his unfamiliarity with that particular evening chore.

While we were out of the house, "Santa" came. Mother said she had heard a noise in the front room and I should go there to investigate. Father said that he too had heard something outside just as we came in. I was easily able to spot a toy or two and some candy and fruit hidden around the front room where "Santa" had made little attempt to conceal them. My childish refrain for months, and even years after was, "Santa came while Mother was beating eggs, and Daddy and I were gathering eggs." The toys I received included a toy tractor and a toy truck. At this writing I still have those toys among my keepsakes somewhere.

My First Move

The owner of the farm where my father worked was an older man, William (Bill) Hobbs. He decided that he would retire from farm work and sell the farm. It was early in the depression and there were signs that things would get even worse. Father had to find work someplace else. He heard of an opening with another farm owner who had a bigger farm and had cattle as well. The man, Charles Nuttle, hired Dad and we moved.

The new house was a very small bungalow (tar paper shack, to be exact), right on the banks of the Walnut River. It had been moved there from the oil fields, where that kind of structure served as temporary housing for workers. The former residents had not been very clean. I remember my mother spending days upon days scrubbing and cleaning. The biggest problem remaining was the bed bugs. These pests were almost impossible to get rid of. I remember that it involved bug spray and gallons of kerosene. Mother meticulously cleaned the bedding; then we set the bed legs in cans of kerosene to keep the bugs from crawling out of the cracks in the wooden floor and the walls, to re-infest the beds.

It was several months before we would visit anyone or permit anyone to visit us because of concern for infecting someone with bedbugs. Mother felt that it was very shameful to have these little blood sucking insects in the house. She equated them to head lice, which she was also repulsed by. For years after, the family would refer to that house as "The Bug House." This was only mentioned when we were among family, or the most intimate of friends.

The house smelled of kerosene for a long time, and it was very fortunate that no one smoked in the house. The fuel soaked floors and walls would have gone up in a puff of smoke with all that accelerant poured around. It was also late spring, so no fires were required except for cooking, and this was done on a small kerosene stove. We did have kerosene lamps in the house for reading and other illumination, but I remember that Mother and Dad cautioned each other about dropping a match when lighting a lamp.

The Ice Man

It was here that I first was introduced to the concept that ice could be used for more than making homemade ice cream. Often in the Summer we would get a small block of ice from the ice house in town and wrap it in sacks to keep it from melting until we got home to make hand-cranked ice cream with an old freezer. It was my job to crank until I got tired or the ice cream became too frozen to turn easily. The ice cream was always delicious, but I always got a headache from eating it because it was so cold.

In any case, we finally purchased a small used ice box, and the ice man began making weekly deliveries of blocks of ice. I remember how great cold milk and iced Kool-Aid tasted on a hot day. I was also terribly fascinated by the ice man with his tongs and picks and his wide leather shoulder cover and apron for handling the ice. I thought what an adventure this must be to travel around the countryside, and deliver such a delightful product.

Gooseberry Picking

Since this new house was near the woods, Mother often took advantage of this by picking gooseberries for pies and canning. Gooseberries were a delicacy at our house. Father liked the pies and we often put gooseberries on our breakfast oatmeal. I don't know why we liked them so much since they were so sour. Perhaps it was because they were such a precious commodity, requiring so much labor to produce. First came the picking, the stemming and washing, then the cooking and adding of tons of sugar to make them at least tolerable to the taste. It took a lot of work for one pie.

I remember on one such trip to the woods. I was along with my mother as usual, and was soon tired of helping to pick. I did not like to help pick gooseberries. The bushes were so prickly that I was always sticking my fingers or snagging my clothes and the berries were so small that I felt that it was a never ending process.

My picking soon turned to play and I wandered off to find things to do that were more exciting than picking berries. I found a tree that was small enough for me to climb, with branches growing just right to allow me to get several feet off the ground. I found a convenient fork in the tree to lean against and spent a while playing lookout for an imaginary band of Indians.

Soon growing tired of this, I started to make my way down from the tree. I had moved one or two limbs down and was looking for the next step when I saw a snake coiled around the trunk of the tree below me. The tree was small enough, and the snake was long enough that he could coil around it and move upward.

I quickly did the bravest thing that I knew how to do. I grabbed the tree tightly and screamed for my mother at the top of my voice. I was too panicky to even attempt to climb back up higher, I simply froze.

Mother was some distance away, but arrived very quickly. She seemed somewhat amused at my predicament, but her hatred of snakes soon took over and she began to look for a stick or fallen branch to kill it. It took her a bit to find a stick, it seemed like forever to me. By this time, the activity made the snake decide that it did not wish to go higher and was making its way back down the tree.

Mother came with a stick and hit the snake until it no longer resembled a snake or anything else but a pulpy mass. She then helped me down from the tree. I was still too petrified to climb down by myself. I remember that I stayed close to Mother the rest of the afternoon and was very dutiful about picking my share of gooseberries.

Thanks Gets Two

Whenever someone didn't thank me for some favor or gift, it always reminded me of an object lesson I learned from my mother in an interesting way. It was Christmas time, and Mother and I were in town for the Santa Claus parade. After the parade, children were allowed to file through a trailer parked on the street. It was here that Santa was located. Each child was to get a candy cane and have about two seconds to ask for one item he or she wanted for Christmas.

I had just turned four by a few days and was small enough that Mother accompanied me. As I got to Santa he handed me a candy cane. Since I was too shy or tongue-tied to say anything, Mother said, "Thank you." Santa Clause then handed Mother two candy canes and said, "Thanks gets two."

She was embarrassed, but took the two canes. She remained sort of red faced for a while. I always remembered the power of thanks (you get two). In later years I came to realize that behind Santa's beard was simply some young guy flirting with Mom. At that time she was 23 or 24, slim, and not bad looking.

CHAPTER THREE:
LIFTOFF

AT LIFTOFF, **A** space vehicle begins a slow wavering ascent into the stratosphere. At this point many things can go wrong. And so it is with children in their formative years. If the early stages are not entered into smoothly or they are off course, the "vehicle" may behave erratically, and the mission may have to be scrubbed, or worse, the equipment may self-destruct. The need for proper guidance is essential at this point. I was now old enough for school.

Happy Valley School

I started school when I was five years old. I would turn six early in the school year, but the teacher was not sure that I was old enough. I remember that she visited our house before school started in order to evaluate me. My mother put me through my paces as I showed off for the teacher, Miss Stark. I knew all of my ABCs, could spell my name, and I spelled the teacher's name on my circular alphabet board.

My performance was the result of continued attention by my mother to my education. She had taught me the alphabet, how to write, and some rudimentary arithmetic. She instilled a love of books and reading by reading to me long before I ever realized that she was reading to me. She also read to my father. I yet remember that they would buy a dime Western novel on the weekend when shopping, and Mother would read it aloud to my father and me, sometimes until Mother's eyes were so heavy that she could hardly hold them open. There were no demands that I go to bed at a certain time. When I fell asleep, I was put to bed.

The school was called Happy Valley. This always seemed very funny to me, because the school house was on the top of a small hill. This small, white, school house was typical of the many one-room schools that dotted rural Kansas. The entire student population was made up of three girls and two boys. The other boy, Jack Tice, was in the eighth grade and hardly recognized my existence. Georgiana Bennington was the only girl in my grade. There was always the adult banter about us, that we were more than simply schoolmates and other such sticky sweet fantasies.

I was not yet attuned to proper school regimen, and I would often get into trouble for not paying attention. The worst of all punishments was evoked; I would have to sit with a girl. This was possible with the long, old fashioned desks that would hold three pupils if need be.

Sometimes, after a long period of good behavior, I would get one of the best rewards. I would get to "dust the erasers" during the last part of the day. Since the chalk boards got a lot of use, as opposed to paper and pencils, the erasers were in need of almost daily beating to remove the chalk dust. It meant nearly a half hour alone outside, while the unlucky students had to study. Mother was always quick to notice my good luck when I came home. I would be covered with chalk dust.

A note about one room school houses should be in order. They accommodated students in grades one through eight. The heat was provided by one huge wood or coal fired stove in the middle of the room, which the teacher was required to start every morning and keep it stoked throughout the school day.

The teacher was also the janitor, and was required to provide many of the teaching materials. The teacher also made sure the children were properly dressed for outside play in bad weather, and tied a lot of shoes and buckled a lot of overshoes for those children who were too young to get the job done properly. She was also the umpire for the organized games, although during the early years there were never enough students for any team sports. The teacher also helped teach hygiene and other common social requirements that might be lacking in a rural setting.

A Great Christmas

That first Christmas at the "bug house" was a great one. It was one in which I received some of the best presents of any Christmas I ever had as a child. My Uncle Kenneth gave me a small Erector set which kept me entranced for years to come. I also received many other toys. One of the toys, a jumping jack, I still have among my souvenirs, nearly eighty years later. Most of the toys were from "Santa", since my parents had a little more money to spend. It was not just the toys that made it a good

Christmas. Everyone seemed in good spirits, the weather was mild and all was right with the world. My Uncle Kenneth was just married and I think that this was the first time that he and his new wife, Clara, had visited us. They came loaded with presents, food and drink for all, and the mood was very festive. I believe that Father opened up some of his precious home brew, and as that got passed around, the mood became even more festive.

With regard to the Erector set, I liked it so well that, in later years when I could afford it, I bought the biggest set they made. At that advanced age I didn't play with it much, but it was a rebellion against not having a bigger one as a child.

Home Brew

Around this time, as a fallout of Prohibition, my parents had begun the practice of making beer at home. The process was simple enough. All it took was a large stone jar, ten gallons of water, ten pounds of sugar, two cakes of yeast and a can of baker's malt, then let it set in a warm place for about ten days. I saw the beer being made so many times that I can remember the formula by heart. One other requirement was a small hydrometer. By using specific gravity, this device was able to indicate the alcohol content of the beer, and thus determine the time to bottle it.

I remember that the recycled ten gallon crockery jar was cracked, but Dad had repaired it with sealing wax. The bottles were all reused as well. They were cleaned by shaking the bottles half full of sand and soapy water. That was one of my jobs.

Another task in which I was involved was the capping of the finished product. The capper was borrowed, but the caps had to be purchased. You could get a huge box of them for very little. I would put the bottle in place, put the cap in the receptacle, and Mother then would fill the bottle with a siphon hose. I would then lean on the handle--Beer capped. Actually, Mother was pretty much in charge of the entire process, mostly by default. The container had to have a spot where it was warm, which usually ended up as the kitchen.

I guess it was my Uncle Steve (Scott) who got my parents into making beer. He was the first one of the family to start it. When Dad saw how simple it was, he decided that we should give it a try. Because of the continued fermentation, and the natural carbonation, bottles would often pop open or explode after they were capped. The worst time was at night when one would explode and wake us up. Father would swear, not only for being awakened, but for losing another beer.

I suppose that the loss of a few bottles was a small price to pay. Dad certainly enjoyed a home brew at the end of a long day. However, he seldom had more than one. On occasion Mother would join him as well. Often, she would only take a half a glass and leave the remainder of the bottle to Dad.

The odor of home brew is distinctive, and we did not want strangers or casual guests around the house. Our code word for making beer was that we had an "Old Hen Setting." This meant that there was a crock of beer fermenting away somewhere in the house. When I would come home from a day at school, the odor of beer would hit me in the face. After a while you didn't notice, however.

During the war, when sugar was rationed, we would conserve on sugar in our food to have enough for the home brew. We would also trade our meat ration stamps for sugar ration stamps with people who lived in the city. We butchered our own beef and pork and did not need the meat ration stamps.

One family friendship was developed through a mutual love of home brew. A traveling salesman for Rawleigh Products, a line of spices, flavors, home remedies, and cleansers, made my parent's acquaintance through his calling upon them to make a sale. He was a roughhewn, plain spoken fellow by the name of Bill Gilbert. He was also a horse-shoeer (farrier) by trade, and it was through both of his jobs that Dad liked him, especially when he found that Bill also made home brew and played pitch. Pearl Gilbert was a very prissy and God fearing woman. She violently hated the limburger cheese that was one of Bill's favorite accompaniments to his beer. One memory of her clearly typifies her to me. When the movie, Gone With the Wind came to town, she was horrified at Clark Gable's line, "Frankly, my dear, I don't give a damn." Our friendship with the Gilberts lasted for many years until Bill passed away.

I remember being at my Uncle Steve's house one Sunday. There were many guests that day. I do not know the occasion. I do remember that everyone was drinking home brew. I was small enough to go from person to person to "take a taste of the foam." There was always a little more than foam in the sip, and it was not long before I began to feel strange. I was rubber legged and wobbling around the room. About this time my mother spotted my actions and screamed, "Good God, you've gotten him drunk." I remembered that she proceeded to berate my father, my uncle and anyone else who had been giving me beer. She put me down for a nap and, as I recall, I did not have any problem falling asleep in spite of all the activity of the party.

Relatives and Friends

My Uncle Steve, who had helped get me drunk, was married to my mother's sister, Helen. They had two children, Ethel and Lloyd. They were about my age and I always looked forward to seeing them. I never seemed to have any playmates.

Aunt Helen contracted pneumonia and died. This was in the days before sulfa and penicillin, not to mention the more modern drugs. It was my first funeral. I remember my Uncle Kenneth taking it really hard, and I asked my mother about that. I knew women cried, but somehow I felt that men were not supposed to do that. Mother said, "It's alright to cry," a lesson I remembered.

After Aunt Helen passed, I didn't see much of my cousins any more. Our families just sort of drifted apart. Only after my cousins reached adulthood did we begin to visit again.

In my early years, my Uncle Kenneth was much older than I, but he was young at heart. He would take me hunting and fishing, teach me how to tree raccoons, how to trap animals, and how to repair cars. Dad was always working and never seemed to take time off. Kenneth lived at home with his mother and did very little work around the farm. That changed when he got married. He also no longer had time to take me places. I gained an aunt, but I lost a fishing buddy.

He and his wife, Clara, continued to live with my grandmother until grandmother suggested firmly that my uncle should earn his keep, so he became a farm laborer to support his family, which soon became three girls in addition to his wife. There were clouds upon the marriage early, however.

When the divorce became final, Clara ended up with the children, but it was pretty much foreordained that there would never be much of a family life for them. Clara moved out of state and my uncle became pretty much dependent upon alcohol to keep him going. He never remarried.

While trotting out the rogues' gallery of some of my relatives I must mention my Uncle Plummer Harker. Plummer was my father's brother-in-law. He had married Dad's older sister, May. She was Father's favorite in his family. Plummer and May had three children: Carl, Edna, and Johnny. May died from complications of childbirth with her last child, Johnny. Johnny was later killed while a teenager. He was shot by a playmate playing cowboys and Indians with loaded rifles.

The children could nearly be called orphans. Their father, my uncle, was a crude, unlearned man, who let the children rear themselves. Carl, the oldest, was a big kid most of his adult life. The little money that he did get from odd jobs was spent on comic books. That was one big reason I liked to visit Uncle Plummer, the house was always full of comic books.

Though my uncle made an attempt to raise his children without a mother, he didn't pull it off too well. They lived in what could charitably be called squalor. Plummer was an itinerant stone mason and could not always be counted on to have a job. The house was ill kept and clean clothes were a rarity. The thing that always fascinated me about his house was the gas lights.

In the early years, he had no electricity, and illumination was provided by gas lights. The lights were supposed to have mantles, but those niceties were nonexistent. The gas jets burned with long tongues of flame licking at the ceiling. The ceiling was sheathed in tin, but I cannot understand why the supporting wood underneath did not catch fire. The gas jets were also left burning day and night because it was difficult to light them and turn them off. With gas for lighting and heating, both of which were not ventilated, I suffered terribly with my asthma whenever the family visited Plummer's house. The only compensation was that there were always stacks of Carl's comic books to read.

Edna, the second child, had few aspirations in life, but did find some gainful employment and she married rather late in life to live to a ripe old age with several grandchildren. One thing I appreciated was that she was a very good friend of my mother's and was a comfort to her in her later years.

With regard to Uncle Plummer's claim to fame, he left his name on the landscape. Many of the grand old stone bridges in Butler County carried his name. Many of the bridges have since been removed because they became too narrow to carry the modern traffic or they were inundated by the two new man-made lakes in the area.

My parents had a very limited group of friends. Nearly all, if not all, played pitch. This is a card game closely related to bid whist. This game seemed to bring out very enthusiastic behavior on the part of everyone concerned. My father was the most enthusiastic. He would bid wildly, bluff mightily, and carry on until the wee hours of the morning. For a few short months Mother and Dad belonged to a pitch club. They won a pair of cheap black vases that somehow, over the years, always found a place of honor in the house. I really can't remember now whether it was first place, the booby prize, or somewhere in between.

I do remember that during the social part of the evening there was much talk of all the men-folk going to New York to find work. This was during the depths of the depression, and they were looking for greener pastures than Kansas. I guess that stuck in my mind because it would have meant another upheaval of the family.

One friend of the family, who is long dead and gone, but I shall only call George, was a study in pathos. I certainly didn't call it that back then, nevertheless I recognized the suffering that George went through. He was a veteran of WWI, and owned a big farm. During the war he had fallen in love with a French girl, but his domineering mother had refused to allow him to marry. As a result he remained a bachelor.

How George met my parents, and thence my mother, I do not know. I only know that he was a frequent visitor and always had little trinkets for me and for Mother. These visits most often occurred when my father was in the fields. There was no hanky-panky; it was an arm's length sort of adulation. I was always present. Somehow, I sensed he hated that. George would often play pitch with Mother and Dad, and we would even visit his house once in a while. Only once do I remember my father sort of rolling his eyes at George's fawning.

One family of friends was John and Ella Condell. They owned a small farm, and used horse power exclusively for planting and harvesting the crops. John also raised a few head of cattle as well, which was probably the source of most of their income. They were an older couple, with one grown son, who had left home and was living on his own. The son, Logan, had gone to school with my mother, and at one time had been a timid suitor for my mother, until Dad's rustic charm had swept her away.

What endeared me most to the Condells was that they saved all the Sunday papers with their comics for me. In those days there were many pages of comics in the paper and the pages were large. The first thing Ella would do, when my parents visited, was to get the papers for me and I would become ensconced on the floor and become oblivious of everything except the world of comic hero's adventures.

Another added attraction of visiting the Condells was that they lived a stone's throw from the main line of the Santa Fe Railroad. The tracks actually ran between their house and their stock barns. On occasion, when rail traffic was slowed for switching, we could by hand signals, entice one of the refrigerator car riders to throw off a block of ice. When we were successful, it meant hand-cranked ice cream for dessert.

Our Economy in the Early Years

During my early years I never remember Father drawing more than thirty dollars a month in wages. However, there was always milk from the cows, eggs from the chickens, a pig and/or a calf to butcher, and a garden plot in which to grow vegetables. There was usually a larger plot as well in which to plant potatoes and sweet corn.

Nickels and dimes were hard to come up with in those early days. The dime novels were precious, as was a rare trip to the movie, even though admission was fifteen cents. I remember one Saturday my mother bought a Chinese checker board for twenty five cents after commiserating with herself over the purchase. When she came home, she cried, and apologized to my father for being so foolish with the money. I think she got her money's worth; she was still playing Chinese checkers with her grandchildren until shortly before her death, nearly seventy years later. This is not a lesson in high finance, it is simply a recollection of things that I remember about buying things that we needed, and put off buying what we only wanted.

Starting with a trip to the grocery store, one must remember that during those early years, there were no supermarkets, grocery carts, coupons, credit cards, and few people used checks. Many who lived in town ran up bills that they paid monthly.

Mother would go into a store with a list and give it to a clerk. The clerk would fill her order, bringing the items to a check out desk, where the bill was totaled by hand with a pencil. Part of the reason for the clerk getting the items was that many items were stored high up on shelves and could not be accessed except by ladder, or what was called an "oatmeal grabber." Allegedly Benjamin Franklin invented that handy gadget for reaching high and retrieving things.

Many fruits and vegetables were sold in #10 cans. These were approximately one gallon in size. The common purchases of our family were plums and blackberries. They ended up on the breakfast oatmeal.

Their attraction was that they were about the cheapest canned fruit available. I haven't seen a #10 can in years on a grocery shelf.

Mother always bought "oleo." We used margarine, and sold our precious cream, instead of making butter with it. When purchased, the block of oleomargarine looked like lard; it was white. The package came with a small capsule of coloring that you would knead into the oleo until the color resembled butter. For special occasions, mother would save enough cream to make butter. It then became my task most often to shake the cream in a fruit jar until it coalesced into butter or, if there was enough cream she would put it into the butter churn. This was a large glass container with a set of affixed gears and paddles. One would turn the crank and agitate the cream until butter formed. My "payment," if I did the churning, was a glass of the delicious buttermilk that remained after the butter was formed.

Another reason for mother's grocery list was that many staples were kept around the store in huge barrels. This included such things as crackers, cookies, pickles, syrup, sugar, nuts, cereal grains, and other things too numerous to mention. These were weighed out with simple balance scales. I remember walking among the many barrels peering into them, and wondering how people would ever eat all that stuff.

In passing, there were no shelled nuts for sale. If you needed nuts you had to crack them and pick out the "nutmeats," which was what they were called in recipes. Of course, needed items for the home were a nutcracker, and nut picks. We didn't have a nut cracker. It was then necessary to use a hammer or pliers, neither of which ever worked well for me. The toughest nuts were the Brazil nuts and black walnuts. There was hardly an easy way to crack those without crushing them. Often that job fell to me, and I would end up with nut flour rather than kernels.

Hard candy was to be found in barrels as well. There were a lot of these sitting around at Christmas time. I always had to be careful not to drool into the barrels. If, on the rare occasion, candy was purchased, it was embarrassing to see the clerk look for the smallest counter weight to measure the purchase.

As to vegetables and fruits in the store, you had only what was in season. There were no cross country shipments. Refrigerator cars did not exist commercially to any great degree. There were some shipments across the country packed in ice, but that made the produce prohibitively expensive.

"Dime stores" flourished. Sewing and craft needs were enough to keep three 'dime stores' viable in our small town: Woolworths, McClellans, and Ramseys. Montgomery Ward, and J.C.Pennys were the go-to stores for work clothes, cheap shoes, and cheap frocks. They sold furniture and appliances, of course, but we never went near those departments. There was only one major shoe store, and two men's stores in town. To my recollection there were only two ladies ready-to-wear stores.

One "dime store" I visited in the summer of 1938, was located in Bentonville, Arkansas. It was to become one of Sam Walton's first stores. It now serves as a Wal-Mart visitor's center. My visit was before his rise to fame. We were visiting my grandmother in Rogers, Arkansas. She had to go to the county seat to pay her taxes or some such business, and my father and I were killing time poking through the variety store. I spotted a small chemistry set that I just had to have. My father gave in to my pleading, and bought it for me. On the way out the door there was a comic book rack, and I saw a new comic hero. I asked Dad for one more dime and he gave in. That comic book was Action Comics #1. A copy of it sold in March of 2010 for 1.5 million dollars, another copy sold in November of 2011 for 2.16 million. I'm sure those were pristine copies, but even the well-thumbed issues now sell for lots of money. I'll never know what became of my copy, but that's a lot of what Economics is all about--grasped opportunities, and lost opportunities.

I did get a suit for high school graduation, but that was as close as I ever got to a men's store until I was making my own money. The shoe store was seldom visited. Shoes were re-soled and re-heeled until there was nothing left of the uppers to which to fasten a new sole. While growing up my parents always bought shoes several sizes too big so I would "get the good out of them" before I outgrew them. It seemed that they were still too big for me when there was nothing left of the shoes.

Overalls were the uniform of the day and my father and I wore ours until there was not much left of them. Mother made her dresses, and later those for my sisters. A "store bought" dress was something you went to weddings and funerals in, and were often buried in.

The Wish Book

A common household companion during my early years was "The Wish Book." That was what we called any of the mail order catalogs of that time. The principal ones were Spiegel, Montgomery Ward, and Sears

Roebuck. We would look and wish. Our desires always exceeded the family resources.

The catalogs seemed almost a connection to civilization. We could see new products on the market, new styles, quality improvements, and note changes in prices, which was one indication of the economy. The catalogs were a sort of education for me. When I had learned my ABCs, mother would have me look up things for her. I'm sure she didn't have all that much interest in all those products, but my looking them up was a learning experience. I also learned to help her figure postage for those things she did order. This, I'm sure, helped my early math skills. The catalogs were much like textbooks for home schooling for me. I know I learned a lot trying to read all about the many items of merchandise carried in those catalogs.

For me, the real "wish" part of the catalogs would kick in with the arrival of the fall and winter editions. Those were the ones listing the Christmas toys. I would spend hours building castles in the air and stocking them with all the contents of the toy section. If we were lucky enough to have an extra dollar or two that we could spend on ordering an item, I would wait patiently for the mailman, and was given the privilege of unwrapping whatever we had purchased. They were never toys, but always some utilitarian item that was cheaper by mail.

At an early age, I was as curious as the next boy, and was often secretly checking the lingerie and unmentionables section of the catalog. I always kept my finger in the hardware section. In case mother came in, I could quickly turn to that.

When we had nearly worn out a catalog from use, it was time for another one to appear in the mail. When the new catalog did arrive, the old catalog was still used, but it had been moved to the outhouse. It resided there in an old basket along with the corn cobs. For the amateur, corn cobs were primitive toilet tissue.

Wash Day

For whatever reason, Monday was always Wash Day. It was a tradition handed down from somewhere. My involvement started when I was old enough to carry a small pail of water to help fill the big wash boiler that was put on the cook stove, and filled early in the morning. Bleach and shaved lye soap were added, and when the water was hot, Mother would add the white articles, such as sheets, pillow cases and tea towels. After they had boiled in the soapy water for a while they would be taken out with a wooden stick and transferred to a big tub of rinse water.

The colored items and work clothes would then be added by turn. When the work clothes were transferred to the rinse water, they were usually scrubbed on a washboard to remove the ground-in dirt and grease. The scrubbing by hand with the strong soap was very hard on Mother's hands and usually left them rough and red. There were no rubber gloves, or skin creams in our house.

I never remember Mother making lye soap, she always got hers from my grandmother. Grandmother would cook up a batch a couple of times a year. Beef fat (tallow) was cooked in a big iron kettle outside the house, over a small fire. It was cooked outside for two reasons: one, the kettle was so big, and two, it smelled so bad cooking. The beef fat was saved up for some time before using it, and it smelled pretty rotten before it had been completely cooked down. After the lye (sodium hydroxide) was added, it was mixed and poured out into big pans to cool and harden. It was then cut into big bars of evil smelling lye soap.

Back to the washing, when I was old enough, I would crank the wringer of the washed and rinsed clothing. From the wash water, the clothes were sometimes wrung out by hand, but from the rinse water they were wrung by the hand cranked wringer.

The next step was drying on the line. Whenever we would move to a new place, Mother would insist upon having two parallel wash lines installed for drying her clean clothes. When I was tall enough to reach the clothes line, one of my jobs was to run a wet rag over the length of the line to remove any dust or dirt that might transfer to the clean clothes. Then I would carry the basket of clothes pins so Mother would not have to bend down while she held an article of clothing on the line to pin it.

Most often Dad would have me carry in wood on washdays after I had filled the wash boiler. I never understood why it was that on wash day I had to haul wood, until I finally caught wise that he didn't want me too close to "woman's work." How sexist is that?

There was even a specific protocol as to how clothing was hung on the line. The whites were always hung together, and they were hung in such a way to hide underwear and other unmentionables from public view. Mother would always pin the clothes together so that one clothespin was between two garments.

When taking down the clothes, mother would never leave the pins on the line. She hung clothes even in freezing weather. Sometimes Father's overalls were brought in as stiff as a board and were stood up near a stove until they would collapse, dried. Shirts, skirts and dresses were always hung by their tails or one side of the bottom hems. This would allow the breeze to blow through them.

Most items were folded into a basket as they were taken from the line. If they were to be ironed, they were left just a tiny bit damp to make sure the wrinkles could be pressed out. Now ironing was another subject entirely, which I knew little about, except to see mother heating the irons on the stove and bringing them to the ironing board and repeating the trips back and forth until the ironing was done.

In later years I was always amused when there was some quiz asking what a bottle with holes in the cap was used for. Well, when mother was ironing, sometimes the clothes were a little too dry to take a press, so she would sprinkle the clothes with water from a bottle with small holes punched in the cap.

Certainly associated with wash day was the mending that needed to be done. Mother insisted on patching clothing meticulously. The edges of patches were turned under just so, and tiny, neat stitches held the patches in place. Sometimes Father's overalls had patches on top of patches. Some people during those times left garments unpatched. That was to let people believe that a hole was an accident of the day, while a patch was planned penury.

In later years Father finally bought Mother a gasoline powered washing machine. It was a contrary thing, and she probably spent as much energy starting and restarting it as she had washing the old fashioned way. Then there was the problem of trying to get the stinking exhaust lead outside so she wouldn't collapse from the fumes (and it still had a hand cranked wringer).

The Circus

At about five or six my parents took me to the circus. It was the big one: Ringling Brothers, Barnum, and Bailey. I remember having enjoyed it very much, but I never had any real desire to see another. I could recall the first one so well there was no need to see it again.

I supposed that was much like I have viewed sporting events. It was pretty much "seen one, seen them all." Of course, if children or grandchildren were playing or acting as a cheerleader, I had to attend to cheer them on.

Regarding amusements, I recall one event that we attended that was not so amusing. In the early days there was a stuffed whale which was being transported around the country on a rail flatcar. My parents wanted to see this "oddity," so we went. The whale was constantly being injected and doused with formaldehyde to preserve it. That certainly didn't stop the odor of the rotting mammal. It was about the most foul-smelling thing one could imagine. Folks with weak stomachs were retching all over the place.

What Technology?

When I was very young it was a real treat to wind up the old Victrola and play the old 78 RPM records in Mom's collection. These were not Jazz, or Blues, or Swing, but orchestral, Gospel, "The Two Black Crows," and an Al Jolson or two. We had nothing on which to play the later 33 1/3 RPM records or the even later 45 RPMs.

Then came the wire recorders and reel-to-reel tape. Naturally we had none of these at home or the late eight-track tapes or the cassettes. These were all of a technology that passed the family by at home. Then the technology that passed me by were CB, Beta Max, VCRs, CDs and then, computers. I had to play catch-up, after I had left the service for a while. To learn everything, I tackled those with a vengeance, and was soon owning the equipment and speaking the language.

There was no telephone in the home until I was in the third or fourth grade. It was a big wooden box mounted on the wall. The phone rang every time anyone on our country line got a call. One could only tell which party it was intended by the number of rings. The family did not live in a house with electricity until I left home to go to high school. The kerosene lamp served the family for a lot of years.

We finally got a radio in the home in the late 40s. What a treat that was. It was battery operated, of course, and the battery was bigger than the radio. The batteries were good for three to five months. The shorter work days of winter meant more radio use. *The Lone Ranger, I Love a Mystery, Inner Sanctum, Gang Busters, Bulldog Drummond, Fibber McGee and Molly,* and *Edgar Bergen & Charlie McCarthy*, were some of the family favorites.

When I bought my mother and father house, and moved them from the farm to the city, my sisters and I shared in buying our parents their first television set. My sisters and I had missed all those cute children's programs which were supposed to help young people grow up. I never had a television set of my own that I could watch until after my wife and I were married. There were TVs in barrack's Day Rooms, officer's clubs, and recreation rooms in BOQs, but they were shared, and I never seemed to find time to watch them anyway.

As to automobiles, Mother and Dad, owned a Model T Ford until I was about five or six years old when they bought their first of about three Model A Fords they owned until they moved to the city. They had no car at all then, until my brother-in-law bought my mother an old Chevrolet. She drove that car until they took the keys away from her. She was getting too old to drive safely.

After high school when I was earning my own money, I started out with an old '38 Chevrolet Coupe that I bought for about $65. It hung together until I joined the service. Mother sold it to a neighbor. It didn't last but a few months before he had to park it back of his hog shed. It was still sitting there after more than ten years. I didn't buy another car until over four years after I had joined the service.

The McClellen Place

Father's boss, Mr. Nuttle, was expanding his holdings and had purchased another farm about five miles away. He offered our family the opportunity to move to the former owner's house on that farm. My parents jumped at the chance. It would get them out of our "bug house" in a poor location into a huge 13 room house on a main road, and it was only a quarter of a mile from a school. This meant another move, but of all the moves we made, it was probably the least traumatic. Even though I was leaving my school mates, we were still so close that we could still see each other occasionally.

The house was so big that we never did have enough furniture to fill more than half of the rooms. Nearly the entire upstairs remained empty. I had much fun in this big house. Nearly every room seemed like a playroom. The third floor was my favorite. It was dry and musty, but its windows afforded views of the farm and outbuildings that I never was able to see before. With no siblings yet, and no near neighbors, the opportunity for imaginary playmates and situations were endless.

Grandpa Garabrandt

It was at the McClellan place that I really got to know my grandfather on my mother's side. He became estranged from my grandmother and came to live with us. He was not a very industrious person and had finally exhausted my grandmother's patience with not keeping the farm running well. He had no head for business or labor and the farm was beginning to see the results of poor management. Grandmother worked as hard as any field hand and tried to keep the place going in spite of her husband. She finally kicked him out and he ended up on our doorstep.

Grandfather was healthy and able bodied, but he did little but sit around, tell me tales, and smoke his pipe. To this day I could not remember one of his stories, but I remember that he kept me entertained at the time. In warm weather he slept in his old car, but when cold weather came, Mother invited him to sleep inside the house. I can still picture him arising late, sitting in the parlor in the morning, and grunting as he put on each sock and shoe. He was a very big man, and his lack of exercise did little to keep him fit.

My father put up with Grandfather for about a year before he told him that he would have to leave. He was doing nothing but eating and taking up space. My father felt that there were day jobs that Grandfather could get to help out the household. With that, Grandfather left and went to live with my uncle, who also tired of him after a year. This time, Grandfather finally got a job and began living on his own.

Teeter School

Although we had not moved very far, there was a new school with which I had to become accustomed. Teeter School, District No. Two, had more school age children than Happy Valley and the school itself was somewhat larger in size. It was still a one room schoolhouse, however. The other thing different about it was that it was red instead of white. There were now three or four students in my same grade and there were students in all of the other grades as well. Miss Helen Bradley, the teacher, was very efficient and got around to everyone with her teaching. She was also able to provide music training for everyone which had been lacking in Happy Valley.

Miss Bradley found time to give me some individual instruction on the piano. I was able to play a simple piece or two by the time we had to move again. I often wondered what I would have been able to do with music if I had been able to have my ability developed further and we could have afforded a piano or a teacher. As it was, we could not even afford the sheet music.

Here at Teeter School, I was first introduced to the dip pen. What a mess! Each desk was fitted with an ink well. The desks here were newer than those at Happy Valley, and only held one student. Anyway, Miss Bradley would hand out the steel pens and pen holders. We were to suck the oil from the pens while she filled the inkwells from a tall bottle. We would begin with our ovals and the vertical strokes from the old Palmer Method instruction books. The scratchy and leaky pens made a mess of the rough paper we used. Writing with ink was not the great accomplishment that most of us had anticipated. The pens were little advanced from the quill pens of the past, and the ink seemed to end up everywhere.

Miss Helen Bradley was a fine teacher, and was loved by all. She was so organized that she was able to give attention to all. At one point she asked my parents if I could skip a grade. They refused to allow it. I don't know why they did that, and I don't know at this late date that it made that much difference in my life either way. Miss Bradley remained in contact with some of her students. I was corresponding with her on occasion up until she was in her 90s.

It was here that I began to miss a lot of school. I remember that I was playing under an old flat bottomed boat near the machine shed at home. The boat was up off the ground, but the ground was damp and cold beneath it. Perhaps this led to my cold, or the mold lead to an allergic reaction, I don't know. In any case, I came down with a bad cold that turned into a kind of pneumonia. From that point on, and nearly for the rest of my life, I was afflicted with asthma. One day the truant officer came to ask Mother why I wasn't in school. She told him that I was ill. He wanted to come in the house to see for himself, but she kicked him off the property.

On The Road Again

Father did not get along well with his boss. The boss was hot tempered and Dad didn't like the way he treated animals. The man would often beat a horse over the head with a hammer for not understanding certain commands that the boss would give it. I remember crying one time when I saw one of those beatings. He was attempting to get the horse to come up to the gate latch in a fence in such a way that the boss could unlatch the gate while he was still in the saddle. I remember the blood running from the poor horse's nose and the wounds on the front of his head.

That was probably not the proximate cause of Father's quitting, but I can imagine that it was one of the precipitating causes. In any case, I was not privy to any discussions of quitting or about moving until someone came to the house one day and talked with us. I remember liking this nice young man who made over me a bit. Dad introduced him as Mr. Eldon Teeter, and said that we would be working for him on a big ranch.

The Ranch

The new home was not that much to brag about, but it was large enough for us. The house was built on a hillside. It had three levels. The main entrance was on the middle level, and a huge labyrinthine basement opened out onto the lower level at the base of the hill. That basement was open and unused. It was well lighted from several windows and an always-open door, so it became my hideaway and playground for years to come.

The house and ranch buildings were all located miles off the main road. The only way in was across the prairie on rutted trails. We got the mail perhaps twice a week at best. Our sporadic trips to the County seat for shopping were usually made on a Saturday. We were now thirteen miles from town and it was not routine to make what was a long trip in those days.

It was on one of these trips to town that we returned rather late Dad had to milk our one cow by lantern light. When he came to the house with the milk he began to build a fire in the front room stove and stayed there tending it. Mother was in the kitchen preparing a late supper. She had only one kerosene lamp burning as she prepared the meal. The light from the kitchen only dimly lighted the front room.

As kids do, I was running from room to room doing nothing very constructive. Suddenly, Dad yelled, "Oh My God, there's a snake in the house." He jumped up and began flailing away at it with the stove poker. Suddenly he shouted again, "Oh, God, he got me."

Well, come to find out, the snake didn't get him. When Mother brought the lamp from the kitchen, the snake had escaped and we found that the end of the poker had broken off and flew back and hit Dad in the chest. He had seen the snake earlier, but presumed it was me dragging something around behind me playing. In fact I had nearly stepped on the snake.

Father chose not to talk about this incident. I think he was a little embarrassed to find that it was the end of the poker and not the snake that had attacked him. After that, mother went around nailing tin can lids to all the cracks and holes to make us not only mouse tight but snake tight.

We would not go to town if it rained, because the rain-filled ravines would be impossible to cross, or the ruts would be so muddy that we would get stuck, or both. If there was snow or a hint of snow, we did not travel. On the prairie there were no road markers or reflectors to tell whether we were on the trail or about to drive into a draw deep enough to bury our Model A Ford.

The trips to town were generally fair weather trips, but we usually had enough basic food provisions to survive if we were snowed in or "mudded" in. Basic provisions included a fifty pound sack of flour, bacon that would keep without refrigeration, sugar, and salt. There were always lots of canned goods in the pantry, either in tin from the store or in glass fruit jars from my mother's home canning. We were now much too far off the beaten path for the ice man.

Writing of the sack of flour reminded me of one of Dad's favorite jokes. If he saw a man carrying a sack of flour, he would say, "There goes a man with a sack of flour on his back, and I'll bet he doesn't have a drop of whiskey in the house." This was a cute joke, but he used it every time. Father did not drink hard liquor. We always kept a bottle in the house for an occasional guest or 'snake bite', but he never imbibed except on special occasions. Even the beer that we used to make, he would take in moderation, seldom more than one bottle at the end of a hard day.

Father's biggest vice was chewing tobacco. He was seldom without a chew in his mouth. There was always a spittoon of some sort by his chair, and when visiting friends, they usually supplied him with a can of some sort. We could be without bread, sugar, flour or salt, and we could "make do," but if Dad was out of tobacco we would go to town, even in a raging blizzard.

Dad's Chaw

If Dad was outside the house, you could bet that Dad had a chew of tobacco in his mouth. If Dad was in the house and not eating or sleeping he probably had a chew of tobacco in his mouth. In the fields on a hot day, he would take a drink of water with a chew of tobacco in his mouth. It was a disgusting habit, Dad's chaw, but it was my father.

In the early years when my father still had good teeth, he chewed plug tobacco. The tobacco was compressed with a little licorice and molasses into hard, flat cakes. It was like a sawed-off board.

Three brands that I remember were Days Work, Horse Shoe, and Old Mule. Old Mule and Horseshoe were thin plugs that had a small tin mule or a horse shoe imbedded in the plug. I got those if I was around when Dad opened the plug wrapper. Day's Work was a thicker plug, but was softer. It had no metal tag. In later years, as Dad's teeth got so bad he couldn't bite off a chew from a plug, he chewed Red Man and Mail Pouch (loose tobacco). I hated that there were no tags, coupons or prizes in any of them.

We could be snowbound for days with hardly a bite of food in the house, and we had to make do, but if Dad was out of tobacco, we harnessed up a team to break a trail to get provisions. Of course, we then could get other essentials like flour, salt, and sugar, which seemed to justify the adventure.

When Dad would quit the fields and come in to dinner at noon, the last thing he would do before entering the house was to disgorge his chaw of tobacco into his hand and give it a flick across the yard. The chickens would pounce upon it as if it was some strange, huge insect and try to tear it apart. As they got the taste of the tobacco they would run about shaking their heads frantically to get the taste out of their mouths. They never learned. They would repeat their attack with the next chaw the next day. When chores were over in the evening and Dad would come in to supper; the chickens were often already roosting for the night.

With that constant mulch of chewed tobacco in the yard within the radius of his throw, you can bet that nothing grew. Once in a while, when Dad had just taken a fresh chaw and dinner was called, he would lay the cud on the porch rail and retrieve it after dinner was over to pop it back into his mouth. There were tales that he once laid a chaw beside his plate and ate dinner, to retrieve it later, but I never saw that, nor was I able to verify it. Mother was pretty permissive when it came to father, but I doubt if she would have let him get away with that.

In the early days, public buildings, law offices, banks, bars, and pool halls kept bright shiny spittoons for their chewing customers. These gradually disappeared over time until the last ones that I saw were in the pool hall. Dad kept a spittoon in the house, but it was not a bright shiny brass one. It was a #10 tin can that blackberries or plums came in. Mother hated to clean that ugly smelly can, but it was one more burden about which she didn't complain much.

Other than wearing them away from chewing on the tobacco, Dad's teeth were sound. I did not know him to have any decays, however, his gums eroded from the tobacco, and he lost his teeth that way. They would become loose and ache, then Dad would pry them out of his mouth with a nail. In later years he refused to get false teeth, even when they were at no cost to him.

Dad's ready remedy for bee and hornet stings, and other common maladies was to slap a wet chaw of tobacco on it. He would say, "It'll draw the swelling out." At times I would have rather endured the pain of the sting than have that tobacco juice dripping down my neck. However, to assure Dad, I would say, "Oh, yeah, I guess it's better now." Otherwise I might get another, fresher chaw slapped on it.

Driving down the road, Dad would chew and spit out the window, even in the coldest weather. If you were in the back seat, you should not forget to keep the rear window up on the driver's side, even in hot weather, or you would get a face full of tobacco juice.

As a kid, I would marvel that Dad could tuck away his chaw in his cheek and drink a bottle of beer or a bottle of pop without getting the two commingled, but he did this often. Dad also smoked an occasional cigar, but if it would go out he would end up chewing it as if it were simply a different shaped plug. Though I tried smoking cigars, a pipe, and cigarettes, I never in my life tried a chew of tobacco, not even a taste. As I got older Dad would offer me a chew from time to time, but I had seen too much of Dad with his chaw, and the constant rain of tobacco juice to ever be tempted.

Dad's Hat

When I see my father in my mind's eye, I see him in those overalls and his battered old felt hat. It was this old sweat-stained fedora that seemed to typify Dad. At a quarter of a mile away I could recognize Dad by the jaunty angle of his hat. It generally sat rakishly over one eye in rain, snow, or prairie fire. He could be picked out of a crowd, not only because of his hat, but his size as well, standing only "five – six" in his "sock feet."

He wore that heavy old fedora year 'round, except perhaps, for a few weeks in the dead of winter when he would dig out an old duck hunter style hat with earflaps. That was for weather when your bare hands would stick to a pump handle.

Dad's hat was ever so utilitarian. He would fill it with maize and feed the chickens out of it and gather eggs in it when mother was busy or indisposed. I once saw him water his horse (and my horse) out of it in a remote pasture where there was no pond or running water. He had turned on a windmill to pump the water. On occasion he would bring a baby rabbit or a baby bird to the house in his hat. He would have disturbed the nest while mowing. This seemed to reveal a tender side of Dad that one seldom saw. Once he brought in a whole nest of baby chickens in his hat. The old hen had hid her nest far away from the outbuildings. He brought them in so that the weasels or civet cats would not get them.

One thing Dad never used his hat for was a spittoon. I saw him in some pretty uncomfortable and nearly panicking situations, such as in the middle of shopping in a big store. His only recourse was to swallow the tobacco juice, since he wouldn't spit on the floor.

I refer to "Dad's hat" as if it was the same hat. It just looked the same from year to year. When Dad's Sunday hat was so dark with sweat and grime that it looked like his work hat, Mother would force him to buy a new one, and his only Sunday hat would then become his work hat. That didn't happen very often, and it didn't take long for the new hat to develop a wide dark sweat stain like the other. He would often come home from town or visiting and do his chores without changing from his Sunday hat. That generally led to more a rapid buildup of dust and sweat.

Dad never wore a straw hat even in the hottest sun. He said they gave him a headache. I can empathize with trying to jam a straw hat down to keep the Kansas wind from blowing it off. I always had the same problem

Dad worked around cattle most of his life, but never owned a pair of cowboy boots or a Western or stockman's hat. He didn't like the big ten gallon hats or care much for the men who wore them. His observation was, "all hat and no cattle." This was strange in a way, because he was an avid movie fan of Hoot Gibson, Tom Mix, Buck Jones and Ken Maynard, all of whom wore big, white, ten gallon hats.

He was also an avid reader of "dime novel" Westerns. That was a Saturday treat for him, and I can remember him reading them with his arms nearly wrapped around the kerosene lamp. Often, Mother would read the Westerns aloud for Dad and me until late at night.

One thing Dad would do with his hat was tip it to the ladies. He was unschooled, and pretty uncouth, but he would tip his hat. He didn't lift it with the crown in the European fashion, but would put two fingers and a thumb to the brim and slightly tug on it.

When Dad passed, Mother wanted me to have his hat. I guess I hemmed and hawed and changed the subject often enough that I didn't get it. I couldn't do it justice by how he wore it and I didn't want to be reminded of Dad by having to look at it once in a while.

Mom's Apron

I think that when I see my mother in my mind's eye, it is with her apron on. There were times when she was ready to get in the car for shopping or a visit when she would remember she had her apron on to protect her good clothes. My grandchildren hardly know what an apron is. They simply aren't worn much this day and age, certainly not by my two daughters.

The principal use of Mother's apron was to protect her dress underneath, because she only had a few. It was easier to wash aprons than dresses and they used less material. However, the practical uses were so many it would be difficult to mention them all. It served as a pot holder for removing hot pans from the oven, it dried our tears, and on occasion was used to wipe noses or for cleaning out dirty ears. It carried eggs from the chicken coop, and baby chickens that had lost their mother hen. It carried chicken feed, and gathered apples from the few trees we had. It even carried chips, kindling and corncobs for the fire in the cooking stove. It carried vegetables from the garden and roasting ears from the corn fields.

Her apron was also used to shoo rambunctious calves that had escaped the pen, it was used to wave Father in from the fields, and it made a handy dust rag for a quick turn around the house when company drove into the yard. It was used to wipe a bit of perspiration from mother's face from working in a hot kitchen or in the garden from the hot sun. There were times that she used it to wipe her own tears. She tried to hide that, and I did not actually see that but once or twice. However, her lot even made me feel sad once in a while.

Mother's aprons were mostly made from feed sacks. Grain companies during those years sold their livestock and chicken feed in gaily printed cotton sacks. Mother took pride in her needlework and the aprons really looked nice. Many of my sisters' dresses, as well, were made from feed sacks.

Grant School

The new school, Grant, District 75, was two miles across the prairie from home. I walked nearly every day except when it was pouring down rain. Then Mother would attempt to negotiate the ruts, the slough crossings, and the mud to get me to school. If the rain had been coming down for some time, the draws were usually running full and Mother would have to drive us "upstream" until she could find a place shallow enough and rocky enough to cross.

One unique thing about Grant school was that everyone's last name began with the letter B. We called it the "B" Hive. The teacher's name was Miss Brammer. Four children, in grades from two to eight, were from the Braman family - Aaron, Junior, Eldon and Neldora. Another family with two school aged children later moved into the district. We thought for a while that this would spoil things, but the family's name was Baily. We kept our "B" business going until the next year, when we learned that our new teacher's name was Miss Fast.

We did not play ball, or tag, or any other games in the usual sense. For some reason, we were all into digging tunnels in the dirt and hiding secret treasures, then drawing maps where to find the treasures. We always hated it when winter came and the ground became too frozen to dig. During the icy months we would perfect our maps and when the spring thaw first made it possible to dig, we were outside with our big spoons and makeshift shovels going at it like moles again.

One "treasure" still remains. The school building, coal shed, and toilets are gone, but the old pump and the foundation of the old swing set remain. We got a new swing set, and when they augered the holes, they waited a few days before setting the posts and filling the space with concrete. In those few days we buried a treasure at the bottom of one of the supporting post holes. It remains in perpetuity. When I visited the site forty years later, though hidden in tall grass, our treasure was still intact. The posts had long since rotted away.

The Ice Storm

One late November day, while I was at school, a bad ice storm passed through the area. It rained and froze on everything. The ground was covered by a thick glaze of ice, telephone wires were sagging and breaking and trees were snapping off. By the time that school let out it was very cold. As I left the school, I was surprised to see my father. He had walked to the school to see me safely home.

As we started back across the prairie, I viewed this as one big ice rink and my own private playground. Father took short mincing steps, hardly able to stand up, while I ran circles around him and took long slides across the ice. The closer we got to home the angrier he seemed. I did not try to find out why as I continued to slide and spin along the way. When we finally arrived home, my father slammed the door and said to my mother, "That's the last time I'm going after him at school. He was more able to make his way back than I was." Though Dad hadn't fallen down on the ice, he did bruise something--his ego.

I Take a Winter Dip

Later that same winter, as I was preparing to make my morning trek to school, I asked my father if it was cold enough that I could cross the "Marshal Draw." If this small, spring-fed creek was frozen, it would save me an extra half-mile of walking. Normally, I would have to veer south some distance to find a place narrow enough or dry enough to cross. Father stated, "Yes, everything is frozen. I took a team and wagon across the river this morning when I fed the cattle."

Pleased with the anticipation of a shorter walk ahead, I left for school a little later. When I came to the stream, it was ice covered, but not with the whiter ice I had expected. Nonetheless, I forged ahead. The ice waited patiently for me until I got midstream. Instead of warning me with little cracks and groans, it gave way all at once and dumped me unceremoniously into the stream up to my waist. I had to break the ice ahead of me toward the bank until I was able to clamber out of the water. The cold began to freeze my clothing almost immediately.

I had not taken many steps back towards home before it seemed like I was in the Tin Man's suit from the Wizard of Oz. I could hardly bend my knees and my feet were beginning to become numb. I tried to hurry as fast as I could, with my overalls chafing my legs and my shoes and stockings like one large cake of ice. The sleeves of my jacket, where I got them wet breaking the ice, were also like heavy frozen blocks.

I suppose the only thing that kept me warm was my rage against Dad for having "lied to me" and causing me all of this pain. When I reached home, my cursing under my breath became loud oaths railing at my father. I staggered in the door and Mother, seeing the problem, got me to the stove and began taking off my clothing. She was able to stand my overalls up by themselves on the porch after she removed them. It was only after I was toweled dry that she got a bar of soap and washed my mouth out for using the swear words that she had heard me use towards my father.

I did not lose any fingers or toes, but for years after I could not stand very cold weather on my feet before my toes would start to ache. I never again would believe that any body of water was frozen solid enough to support me. My later inspection of the crossing, made me realize that the deeper water, having been spring-fed would not freeze as quickly as the shallow water at the river crossing where my father had driven the team. Neither he nor I had taken into account the different conditions of the crossings.

It Sure Beats Walking

I walked into the barn one weekend to find my father working on a small saddle. He was softening the leather with saddle soap and then oiling it. He explained that the owner of the ranch had given Dad his old saddle that he had as a child. It was for me to ride to school. Dad said that he had intended it to be a surprise, but this was as good a time as any for me to find out.

My first question was, "Which horse would I get?" This working ranch had about a dozen saddle horses in the string. I began evaluating which one was the fastest or the best looking horse so that I could impress my classmates. The decision was made for me. The horse that was to be mine was the biggest horse in the string. He stood about 16 hands high and was nearly as broad as a draft horse. His name was Shorty. This was because he had an unusually short tail. My father said that he was the gentlest of all the horses and he could trust this horse to get me to school and back.

I really didn't ride Shorty so much as I just sat on him while he took me from one place to another. I was too small to reach the stirrups from the ground and had to rely upon steps, boxes, gates, fences or other means of getting aboard Shorty. It was quite a trick to learn how to dismount at every pasture gate, open the gate, lead Shorty through, close the gate, and remount, using a convenient fence as an assist.

At school, I had to take off Shorty's bridle and replace it with a halter, so that he did not have to wear the bit in his mouth all during the school day. As with many ranch land schools, the school had a small barn on the grounds. It was in a stall of this barn that I stabled Shorty. The school board kept hay in the barn, but any grain had to be provided by the owners of any horses ridden by students. I had to pump a bucket of water for Shorty each noon. I brought him to the well. It was much easier than carrying the bucket to the barn. In addition, he often drank more than one bucket full. The other students lived much closer than I, and did not have to ride, but on occasion one would ride a horse, just to show off. They only did this after I began to ride.

Much later, when I was to help with the cattle, I would not ride Shorty. Father said that he didn't have "a lick of sense" with cattle. Most "cow ponies" are taught to keep the cattle moving forward. If a cow would move out of line or change direction, the horse would move on its own to head them off. Shorty would pay no attention, and just amble along. Dad later told me that Shorty only was able to stay around because he got me to school and back.

The horse that I drew to herd cattle was smarter than I was about herding. More than once he would dart after a lagging steer and nearly leave me in midair. Only a quick grab for the saddle horn kept me from being dumped on the ground.

This Job Was No Cinch

It was my habit to read while Shorty made his way home from school. He knew the way better than I did and I did not need to guide him in any way. When he came to a gate he would stop and wait for me to let him through and we would continue. I would rock back and forth, lost in my story book, as Shorty picked his way along.

One evening, while in reverie or reading, I felt myself tilting to the left (I still remember the direction). I made a grab for the saddle horn and then realized that the entire saddle was rolling to the left. The saddle kept moving and rolling and there was nothing I could do to stop it. I ended up hanging upside down, staring at the underside of Shorty. I finally could hang on no longer and, as I dropped off, Shorty stepped gingerly over me as if avoiding a cow pie in the middle of the trail.

I recovered my senses, picked up my book, and walked after Shorty. I knew enough not to spook him by grabbing at the reins. He probably was not aware that I was not still in control. The saddle was hanging from his back by the cinch that was normally strapped to his belly. I tried every way that I could think of to get the saddle turned back to where it belonged. However, I could not possibly put it back in place. I finally gave up and started walking home, leading Shorty.

For some reason I had stayed a little longer at school than usual. I suppose that I had been playing with the other kids. In any event, my mother was watching for me and becoming somewhat anxious. It was then that she saw the top of Shorty appear over the horizon. At the same time she realized that I was not in the saddle. She became even more anxious in the few minutes that it took for the top of my head to appear on the horizon and saw that I was leading Shorty. Her anxiety gave way to amusement as she was able to see the saddle hanging under Shorty's belly.

The next day I carried a very detailed note to the teacher relating the possible dire consequences of a repetition of such an incident, and instructions in how to cinch up the saddle for me to make sure that it was tight before I rode off in the evening. This also allowed me to loosen Shorty's cinch in the morning at school and not worry about him being so uncomfortable during the day. Therefore, one more duty added for a busy teacher.

I Ride The Fence

I remember that we were at breakfast one summer morning when Dad surprised me by saying that I was riding well enough now to ride the fence. This meant nearly a day away from home riding along the many miles of fence, re-stapling loose wire and repairing any breaks in the fence that did not require new posts. Mother had some concerns about sending me out alone, but I had been with my father often enough to know what to do.

On the morning on which I was to head out, the weather was perfect. The smell of the barn was warm in my nose and the mingling of hay, horse sweat, and manure was not at all that unpleasant. I didn't look much like a ranch hand, let alone the cowboy I felt myself to be. I had on a battered straw hat, bib overalls, and high topped work shoes (no chaps, boots, or six-gun).

I opened the barn door, drove Shorty from the corral into his stall, and got him saddled. I had a box that I climbed on to put the blanket and saddle on Shorty. I had learned how, and was now strong enough, to cinch the saddle tight enough so that it would not slip off. I got a hammer, a roll of wire and a bag of staples from the maintenance shed and hung them on the saddle. Mother had packed a small lunch, which I also tied to the saddle.

As I rode out to the first pasture gate I felt that this was a rite of passage, though I certainly did not call it that at the time. The ride was rather boring. I kept my eye on the fence, while Shorty kept his eye on the trail as we slowly plodded along. There were not many loose staples to replace, so I did not have to dismount very often as we rode along.

About mid-morning, without warning, Shorty reared up and dumped me unceremoniously on the trail. While I was trying to figure out why he did that, I saw the reason. It was nearly staring at me eyeball to eyeball as I sat in the dirt. It was a rattlesnake. He had come out of hiding this morning to sun himself on the dirt cow path. I cannot remember ever moving so fast; half rolling, half crawling, I distanced myself from the snake before I took the time to get to my feet. It was ingrained in me that I had to kill the rattler. My mother was the one that had implanted that in me. She had a hatred of them.

I had nothing to use as a weapon against the snake. In that part of the prairie, there were few rocks to be found except for an occasional outcropping. The only weapon at hand that I could use was my hammer, and it was on the saddle on Shorty. He had trotted off some distance away and was eating grass as if nothing had happened. I walked up to Shorty, took him to the fence away from the snake and tied him up.

I retrieved my hammer from the saddle and went looking for the snake. He was still there as if he owned the territory. I got as close as I thought that I dared and threw the hammer at him. In my nervousness, I missed him by about as far as I threw the hammer. Now I had to retrieve the hammer again. This was a little trickier. To get the hammer, I had to get much closer to the snake that I had been before.

I circled the snake warily until I could maximize my distance from the snake and minimize the time it would take me to grab the hammer again. I grabbed the hammer and tried again - and again - and again. It took me four or more tries before I was able to injure the snake enough to move in for the kill, which took several more hammer throws.

I now took some time to cool off. I was wringing wet with sweat, made up from fear, exhaustion, and exhilaration. When I could breathe normally, I collected my trophy. I cut off the rattles and put them in my saddle bag and hung the snake on the fence. This was a large snake, well over three feet long. The rattles would look good added to my mother's jar of rattles that the family had collected over the years.

I untied Shorty and we continued down the trail. This time, I kept one eye on the fence and one eye on the trail. I certainly did not want to get dumped again. I might not be so lucky the next time. The rest of the day passed uneventfully. The lack of stapling and wiring jobs made up for the time lost with the snake, and I got home at a reasonable hour.

When I got home that evening I tried to be as casual about the incident as I could. I did not tell anyone or show off the rattles until after dinner. It was all I could do to contain myself. However, though I began slowly and matter of fact about what happen, the further I got with my story the more breathless I became. I nearly began reliving the anxiety and tension. It was somewhat contagious with my mother, who by the time I finished my story, was telling Dad that I was not to go out alone again. Dad grunted and proceeded to examine the rattles, telling me how old the snake was from the number of rattle buttons it contained.

In years to come, the incident would become just another routine occurrence in a day on a ranch, and I rode the fence and helped herd cattle many times after that.

My Sister Becomes the Grinch Who Stole Christmas

Although I never really comprehended that my mother was pregnant, the talk was a lot more hushed when I came around. No one prepared me for having a new brother or sister. Maybe the experience of my mother's last pregnancy several years earlier was enough to dampen any wishful exuberance. I know that I was surprised to find that Mother was in the hospital and Father was taking care of me or leaving me with my Uncle Plumber.

There were several complications, transfusions, etc., all of which I could not understand. I remember my father saying that he was disappointed that he could not "give blood" to my mother, but that her brother, my Uncle Kenneth, could. After Mother came home from the hospital she was taken care of by the Condells in their home for some weeks. I can remember my father taking me to see Mother, and for a first look at my sister, Ethel Louise. She didn't look all that remarkable to have disrupted the family like she did.

Ethel was born on December 17, 1936. That put me as having just turned eight. There were sights and sounds of Christmas in town, but there were not any signs of Christmas activity at home. So with Mother not expected home until after Christmas, all I could hope for was that Santa Claus didn't forget me. I remember coming home with my father early on Christmas Eve, so that he could do the milking, feed the stock and do other evening chores.

In the midst of his rounds he came to the house and rummaged through a few drawers. He came up with a book and some candy. He said, "Son, this is your Christmas." I then asked, "But what did Santa Claus bring me?" He was momentarily at a loss for words and mumbled sheepishly that he guessed that was it. The grim fact finally penetrated my little pea-brain. Santa was my parents, and vice versa. Father went about his chores and I had a quiet time alone to wipe away a few tears of childhood lost. I then found the perfect scapegoat. It was all my sister's fault. Had she not come upon the scene, I would still have the Santa Claus dream to cling to.

The book my parents had given me for Christmas was "Oliver Twist," a big, beautiful, hard bound edition. I was always proud to show it off. I always, said, "Look at what Mom and Dad got me for Christmas." However, to this day, I have not read the book. In addition, for some reason during my life, I have somehow avoided any book, play, or movie based upon that particular Dickens story. More psycho-babble? Who knows.

We Lose Our Boss

The owner of the ranch was a relatively young man. My father liked him very much since he was always willing to work as hard as my father. He was always doing just a little bit more than a normal absentee ranch owner would do. He did not live on the ranch, but he came out often and worked hard. He did not simply let a foreman (my father) and other hired hands do all of the work, he worked as well. His name was Eldon Teeter.

Since he had inherited the ranch from his father, Eldon had slowly begun to make many improvements upon it. His first step toward making a working ranch out of it was to hire my father. He then experimented with various kinds of cattle that would do best before shipping them to market. He tried whiteface cattle, Brahmas from Mexico, and even buffalo.

He also experimented with various kinds of cattle feed and ways to feed the cattle. He made ponds and drilled wells for water. He remodeled the ranch house and outbuildings and purchased new tractors and machinery. He also had my father begin constructing five-wire barbed wire fences with solid hedge posts along all fence lines. It would have been a ranch to be proud of had not Eldon been injured in a fatal accident.

Eldon was strong and well built. His strength, according to my father, was what led to his death. Eldon and my father were falling large trees to clear land and to provide firewood for our house for the winter. In the process of cutting one tree, a huge limb became lodged against a tree. Eldon attempted to dislodge it by lifting it up away from the tree. It twisted out of his hands and fell on his head, fracturing his skull. He did not lose consciousness, and at the house my mother attempted to clean him up, not realizing he was as badly injured as he was. Father raced Eldon to the hospital in town in Eldon's car. He remained conscious for some time at the hospital, but evidently pressure on the brain from his injury caused him to lapse into a coma that evening, and he died during the night.

The Teeter family kept the ranch going for several months after Eldon's death, but they finally made arrangements to sell it. This meant that we would again have to move. My sister was not old enough to have any fond memories of the ranch, but it was very heart wrenching to me to have to leave. It was leaving the surroundings and Shorty more than leaving friends. My schoolmates were so remote by distance that I seldom saw them anyway, except in school.

My father got a job with a Mr. William Condell, who ran a thoroughbred Herford ranch. He said that he could always use a man who knew cattle. Dad got the job through Mr. John Condell, brother to William. John was a lifelong friend of my parents. It was with this couple that my mother stayed after she came home from the hospital with Ethel, my sister.

The Condell Place

Our new home was nicely built and comfortable, but the location was not the best in the world. It was not as far from everything as our home on the ranch, but it was very close to a busy railroad track. It was the Santa Fe main line and it seemed that trains were going each direction at all hours of the day and night. Much to our surprise we began to sleep through the noise of the trains and their passing did little more than cause us to raise our voices when we were awake.

This brings to mind the old saw about a family who lived near the rail line. The trains would come by regularly and wake them up until they became accustomed to them. Then one night the train did not come by on time. The wife woke up, shook the husband, and said, "What was that?"

My agony of being displaced was soon ameliorated by the fact that I was returning to the first school that I had attended, Happy Valley. There were only two students remaining of those who attended when I first went to school there, Lois Fields and Georgiana Bennington.

The school did not seem to have changed a bit. It still had the same wide, three person desks, the ink wells, the old maps and globes and the same books in the library, even though some years had elapsed. Time had stood still for Happy Valley.

It does not seem to me, in retrospect, that we stayed here very long before we were on the move again. There were few events that were very memorable. In school I finished the fourth grade and went through the fifth grade at Happy Valley. I spent most of my time reading and day dreaming. It was during this period that I got my first glimmer of the "facts of life" from an eighth grader at school. I found that boys and girls were built differently after my sister was born, but I didn't find out why, until this time, several years later.

It was during this time that my maternal grandmother, Daisy, came to live with us. After she had divorced from her first husband, she had remarried to Mr. M. J. McCall. She made the connection through a lonely hearts club correspondence courtship. They had eventually sold the farm in Kansas and purchased one in Arkansas. Around this time, M.J. became ill with prostate cancer and died shortly thereafter. After the funeral, we made a trip to Arkansas and brought back her car and some of her belongings, while she closed up the house there. She stayed with us for the time that it took her to write to the lonely hearts club again, and to locate husband number three.

The man she found this time was not a wheeler and dealer like the last one had been. Robert C. Knox was an artist and a dreamer. He also was not very productive with helping to put food on the table. He would rather draw and write. The problem was that grandmother was a catch only in regards to the fact that she had money. Though she was a wonderful person, I believe that much of her attractiveness, because of her humped back, lay in her money. None of her husbands were very industrious, or worth very much, so she continued to support them throughout. She eventually outlived the last one as well, and spent her declining years living with her widowed daughter, my mother.

The Grant Place

For whatever reason, Father severed his relationship with the Condell ranch and began looking for another job. He found that a lawyer, Mr. E. W. Grant, was looking for a hired hand to run his farm. We drove out, looked the place over, and Dad took the job.

The Grant place was strictly a farm. The only cows were milk cows, and the only horses were draft horses. The farm was more a hobby than anything else for Mr. Grant. He had a small cabin where he and his wife would stay on occasion. They planted a garden and would tend it. Mr. Grant would often drive out from town most evenings and help Father milk and do other chores. The milking was quite a job, because there were always twelve or fourteen cows to milk. After milking, the cream was separated in a hand cranked cream separator and the skimmed milk was given to the hogs. Mr. Grant raised lots of hogs.

The house was big enough that we could spread out a little. I had an upstairs bedroom that I could call my own and it had space for my chemistry sets, erector set, books and papers. The heat from the room was provided by the stovepipe from the big heating stove in the room below. It ran up through the floor of my room then into the chimney. It didn't provide much warmth, and did not prevent water from freezing in the room or snow from coming through the cracks, but it took some chill off. The deep feather "tick," with heavy quilts on top, was what really kept me toasty in the winter.

It was here that I was exposed to a lot of things that I had not done before. I learned how to milk cows, how to harness a draft horse, how to rake and stack hay and any number of other jobs around a farm that needed to be done. All of the jobs were fun in learning how, but soon became boring when it required a lot of repetitive kinds of activity.

There was a lot of the farm machinery that I learned to operate. I was now big enough to start the tractors by myself and run some of the machinery. Mr. Grant even hired me after a time to plow the fields when they were a little behind with the work. It was a lot cheaper to hire me than an adult day laborer that he would have had to bring in to do the same job. If he had known, he could have got me to do the job for nothing. I really liked to plow. I could let the tractor chug along with little effort on my part, and I could be lost in day dreams with not too much danger of making a mistake.

I did like to rake hay and we had one old team of horses that were pretty docile. The only problem was that the hay field always gave me an attack of asthma because of the grass pollen. For that matter there were a lot of dusts and pollens that gave me problems, and there were occasions that I really suffered.

The Hay Field

Nearly every farm or ranch had a hay field, a large acreage plot of uncultivated land devoted to growing native grass for feeding the livestock during fall and winter seasons. Back in the day, the hay was preserved by stacking it in the hay field, and using it up a wagon load at a time in winter.

After hay stacks, came hay bales, which compressed the hay into tight wire-tied bundles. Then came the machinery which rolled the hay into tight twine-tied rolls for pickup in the field by tractor or pick-up machinery. There may be new hay stacks now, but they are surely rare indeed.

Haying time was a time of intensive activity on a farm or ranch. All the horses and manpower were in the hayfield at the same time. The horses powered mowers, hay rakes, buck rakes, and the stacker. The mowers cut the grass, the rakes simply lined up rows of cut hay so the buck-rakes could gather it for depositing it on the fork of the stacker. Note that grass becomes hay upon being cut.

The stacker was a crude device that hoisted the hay into the air by means of a horse drawn pulley arrangement. It threw the hay into a high arc onto the stack. As the stack grew higher, the arms of the stacker were extended by moving pins in the arms.

The haystack was simply pile of hay placed and compressed by manual labor. The hay was arranged so best to shed water in the event of rain and snow. Water in the interior of the stack would cause the hay to mold. This moldy hay was unhealthy for livestock if they could even be enticed to eat it.

For some reason it always seemed that my father was the man on top of the stack doing the placing of the hay. To get up and down from the stack, he simply rode the stacker.

As soon as I was old enough to drive a team, I was called to help out in the field. It was not a very demanding job. I only had to guide the horses without falling off the seat of the rake, and trip the rake so that it would dump the hay in a straight row. That was the problem. I never could seem to time the tripping of the lever just right, so the rows were never straight. As my father would say, "It would break a snake's back to crawl along one of your windrows."

When not raking, I would sometimes drive the team that lifted the stacker up with its load of hay. The horses only had to pull forward a short distance to lift the load and then back up to lower the stacker back to ground level. I did not know how to look at the stacker and judge where to stop the team, so my father would make a big mark on the ground for me to give the team the order to "whoa." Otherwise, I might throw the stacker over the stack or damage the pulleys. Aside from the occasional sting from ground dwelling bumble bees, the smell of new mown hay, and the outdoor adventure nearly made the job enjoyable.

A few years later I worked for a short time tying bales being extruded from one of those new-fangled balers. This time we were baling alfalfa instead of hay. That job was dusty and dirty, and I was hard pressed to get the wires tied before the next bale came by.

I was older now and could just barely handle a bale with the aid of a hay hook. The bales nearly weighed as much as I did (some, more), but I managed to load a few before I would give up and get on the wagon to stack bales, rather than lift them from the ground to the wagon.

Compressing hay or alfalfa into bales allowed nearly three to four times the fodder in the same amount of space. This made it more convenient to store and to deliver to livestock than loose fodder. After most things were mechanized, a lot of drudgery was taken out of many farm activities. By that time, however, I was long gone from the farm.

Cole Creek School

The new school was the biggest I had attended so far. Not only was it a large brick structure with two floors and two classrooms, but it had a very large student population. Three or four other districts had merged with Cole Creek. Most of the students were bused to school. There were two bus routes bringing students to this school.

Something new to me was the fact that the "upper room" teacher was a man, Mr. Zimmerman. I had had women teachers for so long that I did not know what to expect from a man. I found that he was willing to punch out some the big farm kids when they became aggressive to him. I also remember him pulling me erect in my seat by the hair of my head for not paying attention.

There were enough kids that we had organized sports, which was also new to me. We competed with other schools in the same "Class A" league throughout the County. We had pretty good success. Many of the students were corn fed farm boys with the strength to run, hit and throw with the best of them. I played on the basketball team, but I warmed the bench more than I participated on the floor.

When I entered the school I was in the sixth grade. There were three other students in my class. I was certainly glad that I did not have to start in the lower room. The teachers seemed to be pretty basic in their approach to the lower grades, much more than they had been at the other schools that I had attended.

While at Cole Creek, the school board decided to add a little culture to the curriculum and hired a music teacher of sorts. This gentleman had convinced several other schools as well that their students needed music to enrich their otherwise drab little lives.

The teacher would visit the school once or twice a week, and for three hours would teach the students in their chosen instrument. For those undecided, the teacher would select an instrument for them so there would be a balance of string, brass and percussion, instead of more than half trumpets.

The entire student body was to participate and all were to work toward the final "concert." Just incidentally, the music teacher had most of the instruments for sale. My parents scraped up enough money for a used violin, and then I spent six months sawing away in practice to try to get something besides the sound of a crying cat out of it.

The grand graduation concert was held at the end of school that year. The only personal reminders I have of all that effort is a dusty violin on top of the bookshelves in the den and a 78 rpm wax record. On the disc is one fuzzy song, and the students stating their name and the instrument they played. I have never played it but once or twice. The playing was terrible, the record is fragile, I don't sound like myself, and there is no device in the house that will play 78s anymore. So much for my musical career.

I can't remember how I met Virginia Smith exactly, but I do know that my parents and her parents became close friends later. She was fascinated by the few simple chemistry "experiments" that I performed for her. Woman's wiles or truth, she seemed to like the fact that I was well read about almost everything. She told her mother that she "loved me for my mind." I liked her for her body. She was pretty and petite, with dark curls hanging nearly to her shoulders.

She was a welcome change from the blond butterballs that were most of the girls. The problem was that she was three grades below me in school. That was an almost insurmountable gap in grade school. You could not fraternize with the "children" and maintain any respect among your classmates. We had a very low key relationship, even away from the school. We never went to any functions together and never had what could reasonably be called a date until after I entered high school. Our respective parents had high hopes that something serious would develop here, but once Virginia entered high school, we ended it after a few dates, primarily because I was just "too cool" for my own good.

I had not been out of the nest for very long, nor tried my wings to any extent. I did not wish to be tied down to a relationship without having tasted the worldly delights of other conquests. I was a pig, and paid for it by losing her.

The "Accident"

One day in late fall, 1939, the cattle got out at the Grant farm. We had to call upon resources of the whole family to get them back in. Dad saddled the owner's son's pony, and instructed me to ride into the brush and chase them out. He would then head them off as they came into range of the gates. Mother was to watch the gates so that what few of the cattle were left inside would not get out while it was open for the ones coming in.

The process was very tedious with only a few at a time being forced out of the brush. My legs were taking a beating, since I had no chaps or other protection available. Father was climbing back and forth over one of the lane fences to try to work two different avenues of escape of the cows.

It was on the occasion of one of these crossings that a lower wire that he was standing on gave way and Dad came down astride the post nearly impaling him upon it. He was in such agony at the moment that he could do little more than lie in a heap on the ground for a while.

Mother was frantic, but we were soon able to help him limp to the house where mother attempted to administer what first aid she could under the circumstances. There was a bad scrape on his leg and on his scrotum. However, though the exterior scratches were minor, it was the "contents" of his scrotum that he felt sure had been reduced to a pulp.

I was able, with less pressure from Dad, to get the cattle into the pasture at last, but Dad was out of commission for several days. Whenever he was asked by others about his accident he was always very circumspect about the exact nature of his injury. My mother was even more obtuse about what had happened. Chalk that up to old fashioned prudishness.

How Mother was ever able to put into writing exactly what had happened, I do not know, but Grandmother mailed my Dad a gift from Arkansas a few weeks later. It was a double hickory nut. Its shape was remarkably like that of a male scrotum. It was my grandmother's idea of a joke. She wrote something to the effect that it was a replacement, or something similar. Dad even hung it on the wall where it stayed for many years. Only close friends and family knew the meaning of it.

It was some months before Dad was as active as he had been before the accident. To my knowledge he never went to the doctor for the injury. He simply "toughed it out." That summer, Mother showed signs of being pregnant. I will always contend that Father was simply trying to prove that he was still a man and that the accident had not made him less so. I know that before this, my mother had made remarks to the effect that Ethel was the last child. Anyway, I believe that my sister Carol was not an accident so much as she was the end result of one. Carol Ann was born November 8, 1940.

The Post Graduate

After I graduated from the eighth grade my parents began to wonder how they would get me through high school. Among the many persons from whom Mother sought advice was the El Dorado High School Principal. She asked what she should do. It was like a counseling session. We lived too far away from town to drive every day, and I did not have a place to stay in town except with Uncle Plummer, in what would have been very deplorable conditions. The Principal advised against that, and suggested that I repeat the eighth grade so that I would not lose contact with an academic environment. He suggested that if I stayed out of school for one year I might never go back.

Though I was viewed by some as a freak, and, though it was simply never done, I went back to school in the fall as a graduate student. I was a grammar school post-graduate. The other students didn't know whether to envy me or to make fun of me because I could coast through the classes and not need to do much studying. Additionally, I did not have to go to work after graduation like their friends, and brothers and sisters did after graduation. By the same token, to some, I had been sentenced to do a penance of some sort. They were trying to get out of school and here I was, coming back when I didn't have to.

I was pretty much *persona no grata* with the teacher. She didn't know what to do with me. She simply treated me as an eighth grader for the most part and I recited lessons with the "real" eighth graders. Since it was the same material and the same tests, I made good grades. The teacher was not very original with her lesson plans.

One thing that exacerbated the situation regarding the teacher was that I was absent a lot that year. I worked in the fields both spring and early fall, and ran a trap line in the winter. The teacher used my "excessive absence" as a ploy to reduce my letter grades. Though I may have learned something, I'm not really sure what.

Needless to say, my attendance was not as great as it might have been, but I kept up with my classes rather well. Most of my absences from school were caused by working at various jobs to make a little money in any way that I could. The biggest flap with the school came about from one of my money making ventures.

The Trap Line

That fall, I had obtained steel traps from my uncle, who was no longer active in the fur business, and proceeded to set out a trap line to catch muskrat, raccoon, opossum and skunk. I was doing rather well, and had made pretty good money. I caught several animals, skinned them, stretched the hides, and shipped them off to the fur company. In the next day or two I would get a check. I always held my breath, because each skin was examined and graded before I got paid and I never knew until I received my check how much money I had made.

One morning in midwinter, Dad said that a blizzard was coming and I had better "run" the trap line and trip all of the traps in the event I could not get to them for several days because of the storm. There was snow on the ground and it was very cold, so I did not expect any animals to be in my traps. It was for this reason that I did not take a gun. I wanted to travel light and get back home. I was half way through my run of the trap line, when I came upon one location where I had set for a skunk or an opossum. The trap had a large skunk in it. I was without my gun to kill it, so I searched about for something to throw. Everything was buried under the snow. I then began to look for a small dead tree that I could break off and use as a club. The small tree that I chose was not as dead as I thought it was. It took me some time before I was able to break it loose from the ground and break off the limbs to form a suitable long range weapon.

I now tried to approach the skunk so that I could get a good swat at it. As I raised my tree to take a swing, the skunk struck first. It had a greater range than I had accounted for. Its first volley caught me full in the face. It stung my eyes even though I was wearing glasses. Some of the liquid got into my mouth. The taste was very bitter. However, the smell was a lot worse than the taste.

Having once been sprayed, I threw caution to the winds and waded into the fray for several fast thumps. The skunk had time to reload and fire once more before I finally brought it down. After releasing the skunk from the trap, I broke its neck to make sure that it didn't regain consciousness and spray me again.

I ran the rest of the trap line carrying the skunk. It was very heavy, and I had to carry it awkwardly away from my side. Fortunately there were no animals in any of the remaining traps, and I returned home as snow was beginning to fall again. Mother would not let me in the house. She made me change my clothes in the garage and poured a bath for me. I washed several times, especially my face and hair. I could no longer smell the odor, since I had become so inured to it.

My mother finally gave approval for me to join society, so I had breakfast and walked to school. I was over an hour late, so I put my outer garments in the cloak room and slipped into my seat. It was not very long before my presence in school was felt by all. What I could no longer smell was now permeating the entire school. The smell was on my overshoes in the cloakroom. Evidently I had not done a very good job cleaning them. The principal came after determining the source of the smell and kicked me out of school, sending me home. She made all sorts of threats and remarked that I thought that I was something special to try to do something like this and that she would not tolerate me coming to school again if there was any repetition of anything like this. Other students later told me that it took almost all day with the windows open to get the smell out of the classrooms.

The graduation ceremony that spring was a strange affair. They listed me on the program as a postgraduate. Many School Board members and friends of the family congratulated me upon having the guts to stay in school.

That summer I worked very hard at anything I could find to get a little money ahead for high school. I even had one period of two months where I worked for Charles Nuttle, Dad's old boss. It was with Dad's approval, and I guess he swallowed a little pride by allowing me to work there, but I had to have a paying job, and it was "any port in a storm." Most of the time, I drove a tractor cultivating corn. I roomed at the Nuttles, coming home only on weekends. I did various jobs around the farm until it was time to make arrangements for high school. I knew I had to go to school or bust. I certainly would not entertain a post-post graduate status.

CHAPTER FOUR:
I ACHIEVE ORBIT

MOVING ON TO high school, I felt that I had left the nest. I had broken free, independent, and unfettered by any bonds with earth. I was getting out, up, and around. The "around" portion I likened to an orbit of, if not the earth, at least the center of my prosaic little universe. I had achieved orbit!

High School

My first exposure to high school was not quite terrifying, but it was certainly unnerving to someone like myself from a small school and limited contact with other students. Now I found myself immersed in what seemed like an anthill of seething, noisy, rushing humanity. My innate introversion was certainly given no respite for having been thrust into this clamorous sea of activity. After the initial trauma of finding my way about, I began to mechanically move through classrooms, subjects, and four years of schoolwork. Since I had no desire to interact with the environment, I could concentrate upon subject material, and was thus able to make good grades throughout high school, with little effort.

I made few friends. I seldom crawled out of my shell far enough to exchange more than simple pleasantries. I certainly did not wish to reveal to anyone how much of a country bumpkin I really was, or at least perceived myself to be. It was a case of, "If they didn't know me, they wouldn't really KNOW me."

Most of the few friends that I made were initiated in shop class. It was there that we had more of an opportunity to interact with each other as we moved about in the relaxed atmosphere of a woodworking shop. Another factor was that none were jocks or participated in any of the team sports. This is not to say that any of us were nerds. We collectively avoided those types. It was just that most of us worked after school and/ or drove long distances home, and had little time to devote to outside school activities.

The group of us that were really close were made up of Harold Davenport, Gerald Fetro, Leonard Erpelding and myself. An interesting sidelight coincidence was that my sister, Ethel married the brother of my best friend, Harold Davenport. This was through no intervention on my part. They met and were married while I was in the service.

I have one story involving this group of friends. At the variety store where I worked, there was a girl, Margie, for whom we all had our tongues hanging out. Camping out one evening along the river, and as the cheap apricot brandy began working, we challenged each other to be the first to score with Margie. In the sober light of day we all began to plot our strategies.

Perhaps it was his better ability on roller skates (Margie liked to skate) or perhaps the other three of us simply struck out, but Harold won the "contest." Margie and Harold later married, but after Harold joined the Air Force, some time after I did, Margie ran away with another service man from the same base. My regret at not being able to go to the skating rink more often when in high school became somewhat mollified with that turn of events.

The Fasts

I don't remember how Mother arranged it, but she got me a room at a boarding house operated by the parents of the Miss Fast I had as a teacher in grade school. Mrs. Fast mostly boarded old ladies, but my mother was able to convince her to take me in. Perhaps she recalled to her the relationship with my former teacher. In fact, Mother had been on the school board at that school.

Mrs. Fast was to prepare at least one meal a day for me, which was breakfast. I remember that the Fasts bought whole grain wheat by the bag from a farmer, washed it, and ground it by hand. This wheat, cooked, was breakfast every morning. I never grew tired of this cooked wheat. It was large pieces of whole wheat, which seemed to need little sugar because of a natural sweetness. Sweetness recalls sugar, and sugar reminded me of sugar ration stamps. Mother had to give Mrs. Fast all the ration stamps issued in my name in return for feeding me the little that she did.

The house had one bathroom. With my room on an upper floor of the west end of the house and the bathroom on the east end, I had to go through three old ladies' rooms or go downstairs, through the living room, through the parlor, down a hall and up the stairs, if I needed to go to the bathroom. Needless to say I tried to keep those visits down to an absolute minimum. I hated getting dressed just to go to the bathroom.

In later years, if it was dark and rain was imminent, I would even go out the second story window to avoid making the trip to the bathroom. On occasion I would go into an empty pop bottle to keep from making the trip. I would smuggle the bottle out of the house the next day. Towards the end of my stay I became more careless with disposing of the bottles. Only once did Mrs. Fast ask if I wanted a chamber pot. The agony of the embarrassment of toting that thing through the house was enough to make me refuse.

I would have welcomed the pot on the once or twice that I came home after drinking and becoming very ill. The sheets of the bed took the brunt of that. In spite of washing soaked sheets and airing out the room, Mrs. Fast never said one thing about my drinking. Perhaps she thought that I was being punished enough. My sprees were not habitual and extremely infrequent. I simply could not hold my liquor. I was a sick drunk, not a happy drunk.

During one period of several months, Mrs. Fast moved a roommate into my room with me. He was Mr. Gene Schindler, a blind preacher. He was not as big a bother as was his seeing-eye dog. The dog seemed to take more room than the preacher. In addition, the dog constantly passed an unholy amount of very bad smelling gas.

One thing that I found interesting was that Gene could read to me after the lights were turned out. He read Braille in bed, and would often read his Reader's Digest articles aloud to me.

The Bakery

The first job I had in town was the result of contacts, or networking, or whatever you might call it. My cousin Edna had worked for a small home bakery across from the high school. She knew that they always hired someone to work early in the mornings during the school year, because students were the biggest share of their customers. The bakery closed during the summer months.

Mother and I went to see the owners. They were a little old English couple, Mr. and Mrs. Percy Thompson. They both spoke with a Cockney accent and I could hardly understand them. They made it known, in no uncertain terms, that the job would be hard work. I convinced them that I was up to the task. After all, if my cousin, a mere girl could do the job, I was certain that I could do it.

I may have spoken too soon about that. The job was really tough. It meant being to work at five thirty in the morning and working non-stop straight through until it was time to dash across the street to school. At noon I would rush to the shop, eat a quick lunch of soup, and wash pans until it was time to dash back to school again. Sometimes I would help wait on the crush of students who were buying small pies, cakes, and rolls for lunch.

Evenings were a little slower. I would wash pans and move supplies until it was time for dinner, after which I would go home to my room. Mrs. Thompson cooked a lot of English food, oxtail soup, kidney pie, boiled beef, turnips and parsnips. It was hearty, but not very memorable for taste.

I was not much of a lover of baked goods after seeing how they were made in a small non-automated shop. Mr. Thompson would knead bread dough in a low vat. His ever-present cigar, often unlighted, would begin to drain spittle into the vat to be mixed along with the flour, salt and leavening. This was a general procedure, not merely a one-time occurrence. In the morning, when preparing the kettle of lard for frying the doughnuts, Mr. Thompson would spit into the pot to tell by the sound of the crackle if the grease was hot enough to fry the doughnuts. I suppose the heat was enough to sterilize, but the thought of the matter was enough to discourage me from eating those items.

The Thompsons had a parrot that was their "family." It had a limited vocabulary, the usual "Hello" and "Polly wants a cracker." The one thing that she did differently was to sing parts of an old English song, the most frequently repeated words of which were, "Oh, Happy Day."

To get me to work on time at the bakery, Mrs. Fast would faithfully awaken me every morning for work, and feed me my breakfast. She was an early riser because Mr. Fast left very early for Wichita where he worked in a defense plant.

The Meat Market

As time went on at school I found myself not being able to do my assignments because of the nearly full-time work at the bakery. Not only was the time a problem, but I was not making much money working at the bakery. I began to look around for a job that would pay more. I found a job that paid more all right, but I also had to do the work of ten men and a boy. Joe Brown's meat market had the reputation of going through part time labor very fast. He worked them so hard that they would give up and quit, but I was very determined that the hard work was not going to chase me away.

I did learn how to do a lot of things. Mr. Brown was very ready to give someone a lot of room to learn. First, I became more familiar with driving. Until this time, I had driven a car very little. Most of my driving had been of farm machinery. The old meat market delivery truck really got a workout. I drove it everywhere. On occasion, Mr. Brown would let me drive him to the country where he contracted for beef and hogs to butcher for the market. These long trips, the local deliveries, and joy riding around town, never resulted in my having an accident.

The market also operated a bakery. It had a smaller output, but it was more modern in operation than Thompson's bakery. Sometimes it was my job to wash pans and do cleaning in the bakery section. At these times it seemed that I had not left the Home Bakery. One thing that I was able to take advantage of was the convenience of a cooler full of open five gallon cans of all kinds of fruit for pie fillings. There were coolers full of prepared meats and cheeses, and there was always the convenient "torn" bread loaf and the "damaged" cookie carton. It certainly reduced the cost of my meals outlay. In fact, all of the sweets made me gain weight, in spite of the hard work.

I learned to steel (sharpen) knives, bone meat, cure bacon and hams, wait on customers, repair machinery, and do any number of a dozen other things. When attempting to learn how to cut meat, it came with the shedding of much of my own blood. I was forever cutting my thumb or finger, and once I poked a boning knife through my hand. I was fortunate; one boy who worked there cut his thumb completely off with the bacon slicer. The doctors sewed it back on, however, and he regained limited use of it.

The lifting and carrying were the hardest. The stocking of the store with boxes of canned goods wasn't hard, but stocking the refrigerators was very strenuous. After the hogs and cattle were butchered at a separate location, they were hauled to the store and hung in the coolers. I would have to carry half-hogs and quarters of beef from the slaughter house to the truck and from the truck to the meat market coolers. That work was back-breaking, and my parents soon advised me to look for another job.

The Dime Store

My next job was with McLellan Stores Company, a variety store. Everyone called it "The Dime Store," but even in those days there was little you could buy for a dime. My job here was to receive freight, check it in, examine it for damage, and verify the contents against the invoice, then send the invoice to accounting. I would then stock the merchandise on the basement shelves until it was needed at a counter, at which time I would help the clerks to restock their counters.

I would also serve as a janitor when the store closed. It involved sweeping, picking up trash, washing windows, and oiling the floor on occasion. This job was a snap physically, compared to Brown's Meat Market. I even made more an hour. I began to realize that paperwork paid more than grunt-work. I felt that since I was not working so hard, I should do something more to make a dollar or two, so I began "moonlighting" by setting pins at the bowling alley after the store closed for the day.

The Bowling Alley

The bowling alley was the typical small town alley. It had ten lanes and was the only alley in town. This meant that there was always a lot of league activity going on, and usually there was an opening for a pin boy. Here, I had to develop physical dexterity and agility. Pin boys were supposed to set two alleys, jumping back and forth between them, keeping the pins set up and spotted without the help of mechanical pin spotters.

I was always getting my legs and shins battered from flying pins. One power bowler on one of the leagues was avoided by pin boys like the plague. He was a big man and threw the ball like a bullet, not in a hook or a curve. Pins would fly, and sometimes shatter. One night, I was unfortunate enough to draw the lanes where he was bowling, and was the worse off for it. About the end of the second game, a spare pickup by the power bowler sent a pin caroming off my temple. It knocked me cold for several minutes. When I recovered there were all sorts of concerns for my welfare, but I told them that I was all right and finished setting the last game. I got an extra big tip that night from the bowlers. I wondered later if I could find ways to get knocked out every night and double my take-home pay.

It was in this "den of iniquity," the bowling alley, that I learned to smoke and to drink stuff stronger than home brew. The class of people that hung out here was not the type of people with which I had associated previously. However, it all added to a well-rounded education in the "college of hard knocks."

The leagues were seldom over until after 11 o'clock and it was usually after midnight before I got home and into bed. This left me very little time for homework, but I had learned to manage my time efficiently, and my grades never suffered.

Graduation

When graduation came in June 1947, I was ready for it. School had become very boring and there were no classes that seemed to challenge me. I wanted to get on with my life, whatever that was going to be. I remember that Mother and Dad came down to El Dorado for the graduation. While other graduates were having parties and catered affairs, we went to a bar. Dad bought me a "rite of passage" bottle of beer. To my knowledge he had never bought me a beer before. I had always sneaked a drink of someone else's beer before this. And of course, I had often had my own beer when we were making home brew.

When my friends and I would sneak out during high school, for the express purpose of getting drunk, we would always end up with cheap bootleg apricot or peach brandy. Kansas was still dry, and you had to know a bootlegger to get hard liquor. Because it was elicit, we drank the "hard stuff" rather than beer. We were not old enough to buy beer anyway. The best thing about getting it from the bootlegger was that he did not check IDs, he only counted money.

Anyway, after my "graduation party" I went back to work the next day and that was that. With the added hours, I was now able to have a few more dollars in my weekly pay envelope.

Rocky Mountain High

A week or two after graduation, three other friends and I decided that we owed ourselves a vacation of some sort. With several "study sessions," we decided upon Colorado. We would see the parks, climb Pike's Peak and have a high old time.

The store manager of McLellans did not want to give me the time off, but I took it anyway. With a few days to lay in provisions, pack our bags, and load our cameras, we hit the open road in Bill Wettengle's car. The other intrepid travelers were Aubrey Cloud, Gene Middleton and I.

We made it as far as Garden City, Kansas, before the most God-awful rainstorm imaginable forced us off the highway. We found an ancient hotel in the downtown area. We took one room. It was on the second floor and there were no elevators in this old building. I had never seen such a long flight of stairs before in my life. We had expected to reach Colorado before we had to spend any of our meager funds, but we sucked it up, and headed out the next morning.

We made a quick pass through Denver and then forged on through to Colorado Springs. We found a cheap motel where we could all bunk, and used it as our base of operations. We took in the Garden of the Gods, The Seven Falls and then Pike's Peak. After many pictures at the Peak we headed back down. As opposed to the trip up, this time the car did not overheat.

At one scenic point about halfway down, we stopped for pictures. Returning to the car someone said to me, "Hurry up!" I did. That was a mistake. On the steep graveled slope my feet did not keep up with the upper part of my body and I went face first into the gravel at considerable speed by now.

I had put my hands in front of me to break my fall and laid my left palm open on the sharp gravel. It was not such an ugly wound as it was painful, the hand having many thousands of nerve endings. Using everyone's handkerchiefs, they wrapped my hand up like a cocoon. We continued down the peak and found a doctor's office in Manitou Springs.

The doctor was Chinese. He sewed up my hand without benefit of a painkiller of any sort. I think that I wet my pants from the pain, but my friends cringed and made no jokes about it ... Ever.

He dabbed a big gob of green looking stuff on the sewing job, and sent us on our way. The bill, if I remember correctly, was ridiculously low. After all, he didn't give me a Novocain shot.

We decided we had seen about everything, and we were running out of funds. That together with my accident put a damper on any more sightseeing, so we headed home.

As a further note, I went to a local doctor to have the bandage changed in two weeks as the doctor ordered. When the nurse opened the bandage and came to the green stuff, she stopped and called the doctor in. She thought I had a massive infection. I explained that was what the doctor smeared on it. He said it certainly did not look like traditional medicine. I still carry the scar some 65 years later.

Jail Time

After returning from the post-graduation trip to Colorado with my friends and learning that I was fired for taking what amounted to an unauthorized leave from work, I was hard pressed for money, so I was casting about for a job.

Aubrey Cloud, a school chum, and one of the party in our Colorado trip, went to Oklahoma each year to work in the harvest. He had a relative near Pond Creek, Oklahoma, for whom he worked each year. He suggested that I might find work down there.

So, after dawdling a bit, I packed a cheap cardboard suitcase and took off hitchhiking. I wore my best clothes thinking I would be picked up more readily. Well, a sport jacket is not recommended wear in the hot Kansas sun.

I walked to the city limits to get out on the highway. I was already perspiring by the time I got to the highway out of town. I got my first ride about ten o'clock. It was in a beat-up old pickup. Then I found that he was going only as far in my direction as the next main highway intersection. A whole nine miles.

Around ten-thirty, another car stopped. The driver asked, "Where are you headed?" I told him Pond Creek, Oklahoma. He pulled out a map, looked at it, and then said, "I'm going that way."

The guy was about middle aged, a little stout, slightly balding, wore glasses, and had great smelling aftershave. That's about all I remember about him. The thing that struck me was how clean his car was inside and out. I had never seen a car so clean on the inside except on a showroom floor.

As he drove, he kept up a line of chatter that kind of bugged me after a while. I was never much to carry on a conversation. A little after lunch time he pulled in at a restaurant, and after a bathroom break, he insisted on buying me a sandwich and a soda. If memory serves, it was chicken salad and an orange pop. He had a cream soda and a tuna fish sandwich.

Anyway, we were on the road again after another stop for gas. The guy asked where I was staying the night. I told him that my friend had informed me that there was a rooming house in Pond Creek. He said that the county seat, just a few miles down the road, had a good motel, and that he would help me out if I was short of cash.

Well, at that age, and living a sheltered life on the farm, I wouldn't have known a homosexual if he had been wearing a sign. But this guy was too good to be true. I was suspicious of him simply because he was too generous. The first indication was that he was going out of his way to drop me off in this tiny one-horse town. In retrospect, he made no overtures toward me. He simply may have been doing a good deed. I thanked him for the ride and had him drop me off at the main intersection in the middle of Pond Creek.

It was late evening before I found the rooming house and got settled in. The next morning after breakfast I walked down to the implement dealership, where every farmer and his dog seemed to hang out.

Much to the amusement of some of the guys, I had missed the "harvest." The grain was already cut, threshed, hauled, and in bins. I did, however, learn that a farmer was looking for a tractor driver to plow the wheat fields.

To make a long story short, I found the farmer. He hired me after a lot of questions, and then took me to the rooming house to collect my suitcase. He put me upstairs in his big house where another hired hand was staying as well. The farmer's wife would fix breakfast every morning. There were two young children playing about the house, but I paid them no mind ... My mistake.

Before the day was out, I was in the field plowing. The next couple of days were pretty uneventful, keeping my eye on the last plow furrow as I opened up three more rows of black dirt with each swath. The third day, disaster struck. The front right wheel of the tractor, a big four wheel, John Deere "D" broke off.

There I was in the middle of the field, not knowing how it happened. I had long walk back to the farm house, to explain the problem to the farmer. He was with his other farm hand, so we all went to Pond Creek to find repairs.

While the boss was arranging repairs, the other hand and I went to the local restaurant, beer hall, and recreation center, which seemed a part of Pond Creek's social life. There we each had a beer. They served me, so I guess there was no age problem in Oklahoma for beer.

I drifted over to the implement dealership, the other social center, and hung out for a while. A bit later the farmer (the boss) came in looking really angry. He took me to his car, gave me a check for the work I had done, and handed me my suitcase. Someone had crammed all my belongings from his house into it.

[Now for the "rest of the story"] After several attempts at trying to get the farmer to tell me the problem and trying to explain that the tractor wheel breaking was an accident, he finally told me the reason. He said his children had found a gun in my suitcase! He could not have anyone around that could be of danger to his children. OK, in the cold light of day, I can understand that. OK, so I owned the damned gun. I tried to explain to him that I only had it to shoot rabbits off the tractor, as I scared them up plowing along. Ha! I couldn't have hit the broad side of a barn, from the inside, with all the doors closed.

Anyway, in my senior year in high school I had traded for this small .32 caliber Colt, semi-automatic pistol. I needed it like I needed another hole in my head. It was cute. I had fired it a few times on the farm at defenseless fence posts and trees. In packing for the trip to Oklahoma I had stupidly thrown it into my suitcase with the dim-bulb thought that I might need protection some time so far from home.

[It gets better (worse)] The farmer was having none of my excuses and he delivered me back to the rooming house. Later that afternoon I was in the bathroom when there was a vigorous pounding on the bathroom door. I said, "Just a minute," but the person was having none of that, and kept pounding. I hurried to open the door and there, staring me in the face, was the biggest gun I had ever seen.

Of course, my immediate fright had increased the apparent size of this standard .45 caliber revolver to the size of a cannon. The police officer holding the gun shoved me up against the wall and frisked me in one quick motion and before I knew it I was in handcuffs.

The landlady stared open mouthed as the officer walked me past her to his patrol car. He would answer none of my sputtered questions and took me directly to what might be generously called a jail. It was much more reminiscent of what I had read of dungeons. The three outside walls were of concrete, a foot to eighteen inches thick, the bars on the inside were only thick iron. The only furniture was a rusty iron cot with rusty springs bolted to the wall. The only plumbing was a hole in the concrete floor in the corner. There was one window about six inches wide and two foot high with one vertical bar in the middle. It was located high on the wall.

The "building" had an open area outside the bars, but there was no furniture in that space either. The door to the street was of thick planks crossed with angle iron, with a huge hasp for a padlock. The police officer, who was a local constable, and the only police force Pond Creek possessed, had deposited me unceremoniously in the secure section and departed. There I sat.

I had all sorts of fantasies. I wondered what they were going to do to me. I wondered if Oklahoma allowed flogging. Interestingly enough, I learned in later years that at least one state still permitted flogging until the 1970's.

I sat for about an hour on the rusty springs of the cot before someone showed up. This man was in plain clothes and introduced himself to me as a deputy county sheriff.

I found that I was being accused of stealing twenty dollars from the hired hand that worked for the same farmer for whom I had been working. Well, here was their case: Motive: greed; Opportunity: I slept in the same room with the victim; Evidence: I had a twenty dollar bill in my wallet. Evidence: I had been carrying a gun, and was a bad guy from the big city (El Dorado: population 8,000).

I spent awhile standing at the cell door explaining the gun and the twenty dollars. I had kept the bill folded tightly in a pocket of the wallet for emergencies. The deputy left and I was back to the cot.

Not much later, however, I heard someone trying to talk to me through the high window of the cell. She sounded young, but I couldn't see who it was. She began by asking me all sorts of questions, some of which were as personal as the deputy had been asking. I gave her straight answers, but she was tight mouthed about who she was. Then, without saying good bye, so long, or rot in hell, she left.

Another wait on the cot and, about an hour later, the deputy put in an appearance. He unlocked the cage, and said, "Let's go." He put me in a patrol car and headed out of town. I was afraid to ask where we were going, but he volunteered in a bit. He said, "I'm taking you to catch the bus. A girl at the restaurant said she found the twenty dollars on the floor of a booth this morning, so your story checks out. I guess the hand could have lost it when he was having the beer."

I asked if there was some way I could thank the girl, or at least get her name. He refused. I'm not sure he didn't think that the waitress and I had been in collusion. He then told me he was keeping my gun until he checked it out and would send it to me later. The deputy used his siren to pull the Greyhound bus over, and he handed me a ticket. He made sure I was on the bus with my suitcase. When I turned around to thank him he was headed to the patrol car, and I was "on my way out of Dodge."

Never again did I hitchhike anywhere. Two months later I received a package in the mail. It was the .32 pistol. I was sure that I would never see it again. Years after, I often think of that waitress. What might have they done to me if she hadn't come forward. In small towns it doesn't take much evidence to put you away, especially some young punk.

Montgomery Ward

The very first week back from my harrowing experience in Oklahoma, I made a trip to the employment office. The first day they found me a job with Montgomery Ward & Co. It was right across the street from where I was fired.

The job was initially that of Display Man. This meant that I decorated the windows of the store, partitioned counters for merchandise, maintained signs and banners, decorated the store for special events and holidays, and otherwise ran the display and promotion advertising. This did not take much creative endeavor, since most of the window display designs were provided to the store in packages by the company headquarters. Signs, decorations, and other materials were mass produced and distributed to every Montgomery Ward store across the USA.

I was later moved to clerk in the menswear department. After some months there, I joined a program for management training. Soon after this I became manager of the menswear department. Managing a department added a lot of responsibilities I had not encountered before. One big one was how much of what merchandise to buy for the coming season. I had to order new merchandise based upon how well I thought it would sell. If I made a mistake, and there were items left over on which I had to take a markdown, I would not receive a good rating report. I sweated every decision, but I did not do too badly. Neither did I excel to the point of winning any store competitions.

It was around this time, flush with money from an increased salary, that I bought my first car. It was on old 1938 Chevrolet Coupe, pea green in color. I think I paid $65.00 for it. Whatever I paid was too much even for an eleven year old car. I had not driven it very long before I lost a piston rod. My uncle repaired it for me. Then the brakes went out. Battery corrosion had eaten through the brake rods. This was in the days before hydraulic brakes, and the steel rods that actuated the brakes were subject to binding, bending, and breaking.

The car did not turn out to be the solution to my dating problems that I had envisioned it to be. During the time that I owned it, which was only for a short while before I joined the service, I can only recall but one or two bona fide dates that I had. Those involved trips to Wichita, and to the amusement park there. Since I was no longer in high school, and did not travel in any "social circles," it was difficult meeting someone "date worthy." The car, however, did give me freedom to go where and when I pleased and I did not have to rely upon my parents to give me a ride back to the farm for weekends. Hanging out at the drive-in and cruising Main Street with a bunch of guys was the biggest source of amusement after working hours. There's not much to be said for that.

The Pie Supper

There are some dumb things that you do in your life that make you cringe in embarrassment when you think back on them. The one beauty that I relate here is no attempt to convince one that it was the only, or even the biggest, social blunder that I ever made. It is included only to reassure the reader that I'm human, with human frailties.

The circumstances were that Cole Creek School was having a "box supper." For the uninitiated, a box supper simply means that a girl makes a pie or a box lunch and brings it to the party, where her beaux, or her wannabe boyfriend, bids on it at an auction. The proceeds go to the cause or charity of the moment. The winning bidder then gets to sit and eat his purchase with the girl that brought the pie or box lunch.

I learned that Virginia Smith, my "ex" friend, was taking a box to the supper. Since I was still somewhat sweet on her, I decided to go to the party and bid on the box. Okay so far, but I got the wild idea to bring along a "spare." This was in the event that if I was not the successful bidder, or there was some other problem, I would have a fallback plan. Thus, I invited a girl. I had my car now and did not have to rely upon someone else for wheels. I partially rationalized inviting Dorothy by determining that, as a city girl, she had never been to a genuine, country pie supper before, and this would be her big opportunity to see one up close.

To avoid reliving the event in every cringing detail, I will briefly summarize. I bid on the box, successfully. I sat with Virginia to eat it with her, while explaining to her that the other girl was "just a fellow employee from work." All this while, Dorothy was sitting with my parents, wondering what the hell was going on. My parents were very miffed at my behavior and could not understand why I had placed Dorothy and Virginia in the position that I did. If I can recall, I did not introduce them to each other during the evening. I later rescued Dorothy and took her home, while Virginia went home with her parents. A good time was not had by all. I guess I thought I was pretty hot stuff at the moment, but in retrospect it was a pretty crummy operation.

The Fraternal Order of Eagles

Casting about for "manly" things to do, I joined the lodge of the Fraternal Order of Eagles when I turned eighteen. It was a working man's club, as opposed to the Elks Club, which was a business and professional men's club, at least in our community. In addition, The Elks did not accept members until they were 21.

The ritual and "secret lodge stuff" was pretty hokey, but membership let me rub elbows with adults as an equal, at least there in lodge. I learned to play poker, paying a lot of money "for lessons," but soon I was able to hold my own and stay even over the weeks and months. A lot of the members were attracted to the slot machines, however, I could never get really enthused about betting on the spin of a wheel, which was programmed to mechanically produce exact mathematical odds against the player.

With regards to the slot machines, I was offered a job in the Philippines to service and collect from the thousands of slot machines that this high-rolling "business man" owned there. The natives were crazy about the machines and would line up to put their money in the machines. They would pull the handle and watch the coin return chute, rather than the spinning reels that would tell the payoff combination. They could only understand the money coming back, not the cherries, lemons and bells.

I was to travel to the Philippines as "an Engineer," at least that's what my visa would say. (Ha, me an engineer at my age, who were they kidding?) That was simply to satisfy the country's entry requirements. There were also payoffs being made to certain officials to allow the slot's operation to continue in the islands. The pay I would get was much more than I could ever dream of, but I didn't take the plunge. I learned that life was not worth two cents there, and there always seemed to be openings for machine servicers and collectors. On brightly lit streets, the natives would stick a gun in your ear or put a bolo to your throat, and politely ask you for your collection money. You would hand over the bag and go about your business. If you were a little too protective of the bag, you were relieved of it anyway, but you no longer were around to protest. The other little catch was that you had to underwrite the expense of the robbery. You delivered the money, made up out of your own pocket if necessary. The holdup was no excuse for a failure to deliver the bag.

Later, the same guy that had offered me the job overseas asked me to travel on weekends with him and his crew to various small meetings and conferences around the state, where he would operate several gambling tables. He had craps, blackjack, roulette and poker. My job was to take a bundle of his money (usually a thousand dollars) and act like a local yokel. I was to come in and help build a crowd by shooting craps or playing blackjack and whooping and hollering when I won, or make a lot of noise like I was having fun, even if I was losing. I was a shill. I would get a hundred dollars, my meals, and my room paid for. I did not go on too many of these trips. I'm sure that at my age I didn't look all that convincing as an avid gambler anyway.

The Eagles Club became my hang out and my activity almost to the exclusion of anything else. As an "active" member I was soon filling in for vacant officers at meetings and very shortly I was nominated for the office of vice president. After a year in that chair, it was almost automatic that I would become the president of the lodge. That also was parlayed into the position of third or fourth vice president of the state organization. I thus became the youngest state officer and the second youngest lodge president, ever, of the nationwide F.O.E.

I felt that I was orbiting pretty high. I was "buying" my way into being accepted in the only way that I knew how. My next step was joining the Elks Lodge, the Benevolent Protective Order of Elks. I did this the minute I turned 21 and could find a sponsor. I found a sponsor in the form of the husband of one of my fellow employees at Wards. I did not become a very active member there for two reasons. One, I felt a little out of place, and two, I was not a member but for a few months before I joined the military.

CHAPTER FIVE:
REENTRY

WHETHER THE ORBIT decays as a result of earth's gravity, or whether the vehicle deliberately returns to earth to later embark on another mission, the vehicle must sooner or later alight. It was time to take stock of my life and not just aimlessly orbit about. I needed something that would give me a sense of purpose, a feeling of satisfaction. I had ambition, but no good place to spend it. I certainly felt that I needed some sort of change. I needed to scrub the current mission and come to earth, where I could embark on another part of my life.

At this point in my life I still thought of myself as a boy. I had turned twenty-one with little fanfare and with little change in my life. I still worked for Montgomery Ward; I still lived at the boarding house, and about the only thing different was that I no longer worked at the bowling alley. I did take a class or two at the junior college, but this was mostly evenings and seldom took much study time. I did not want a "degree" at the local college, and I did not have the money to go away to college. I simply bided my time and banked as much money as I could.

My time at the Eagles Lodge gave me little time for any kind of a social life where I could meet many women my age. The girls that I did manage to meet and date always ended up seeming so shallow and immature that no relationship lasted very long.

So I was a drifter and a gambler. Of course, I didn't drift very far, at least not beyond the city limits of El Dorado, and I certainly didn't gamble for very big stakes; I didn't have the money. I was drifting without any real direction. The time was ripe for a change in my life.

The change that I made was rather drastic. It meant pulling up roots, and closing a lot of doors behind me. Probably the biggest change was that of no longer having ready access to home and family. Part of the urge for a change was based on my desire to find a place where decisions were made for me. The tough part of life seemed to be making choices and decisions. Later in life, I learned that there was no such place, and I found that I could be paid big bucks for making those decisions.

For this new phase of my life, the early military years, I thought of terms such as "Induction", "Indoctrination", and "Independence" for chapter titles. Alternatively, I toyed with "Education", and "Expanding Horizons", but those terms seemed only to partially cover everything which was involved. Therefore, I begin with a chapter simply called: "Counting the Days."

With that thought, we shall move to part two of my narrative entitled, "Military Life: The Early Years."

PART II:
MILITARY LIFE: THE EARLY YEARS

CHAPTER SIX:
COUNTING THE DAYS

TWO OR THREE times a week I would walk from Montgomery Ward to the post office at lunch time to see if there were any new stamps to add to my growing collection. This day, on my way back to the store, the Air Force recruiting office caught my eye with more force than it had in the past. Before I knew it, I found myself talking to the Air Force Recruiting Sergeant about a tour in the Air Force. He convinced me that my draft call for an involuntary tour in the Army was about to come up. I felt that the glamour of the Air Force, even with its compulsory four years, was better than two years in the not-so-enticing Army. I was about ready to believe that I would be a pilot with my own plane in a very short time. Before I left the recruiting office I found that I was to be on a bus that very evening, bound for the indoctrination center in Kansas City.

I went back to my boss at Montgomery Ward and told him that this was my last day, and to have my check ready for me that evening. For some reason my mother had chosen this day to come to town from the farm to deliver my laundry to the rooming house. She gave me a call at the store to ask if we could see each other before she returned home. I told her no, that I was joining the service. I would have liked to have broken the news to her gently, but there was no way to do this at this late date. I think that without really saying so, we mutually agreed that it was best that I did not see her, and that she should not see me off. As it was, we were both pretty emotional on the phone.

I went to the rooming house that evening, packed a few essentials, and told my landlady that I was leaving. I said that my mother would be in at a later date to clean out my room. The landlady then told me that my name was in the evening paper for my draft call. However, I had not received the official notice in the mail. After a few hurried good-byes, and leaving my car parked in front of the rooming house, I made my way to the bus station.

The trip to Kansas City was pretty much of a blur. I was lost in my thoughts, with some trepidation about what the future held, and at times kicking myself for acting without giving much thought to this life-changing decision.

We arrived in Kansas City late at night at some barracks type dormitory where we were to spend the night before going to the indoctrination center in the morning. There were about twenty-five men on the bus. Two men, other than me, were from my home town. The bus picked up the others along the way as we drove to Kansas City. As I made ready for bed, I noted how stark and barren the accommodations were. Little did I realize then that this was veritably palatial compared to what I would encounter later in my travels.

Day One

We were awakened at a reasonable hour to find the place a regular beehive of activity. Other busses had arrived overnight from Missouri, Nebraska and other parts of Kansas. We were given breakfast and bussed to the indoctrination center. The numbers of persons had grown to three full bus loads. The first hurdle was the physical examination. Everyone was a bit dazed as we were herded about. It seemed a little like a cattle drive back on the Ranch. We were finally organized into rows of scrawny humanity, trying to hang on to a bit of dignity, when all we had on were flimsy shorts. It was interesting to note that the person in front of me was wheezing a little bit with obvious asthma. I then noted that I was wheezing as bad. I was so used to wheezing that I hardly ever noticed it of myself unless it started to really constrict my breathing. The doctor checked the guy and asked him if he had asthma. The guy said, "No!" The doctor promptly rejected him and told him to get dressed. He asked me the same question. I said, "Yes, but it doesn't bother me much." For some malicious reason he passed me. Perhaps the stethoscope told the doctor something neither the reject nor myself were aware, or maybe the doctor was just proving that you shouldn't tell lies. I will never know.

The physical examination, though very assembly-line-like in its being carried out, seemed thorough enough. After all of the poking and prodding, there were a few that had to take busses back home. After a quick lunch, the next part of the ordeal was the written examination and the classification tests. Those persons in charge in the testing area emphasized to us that the results of the classification tests determined what we would doing in the service for the next four years. I put all that I had into the test, and it took several hours to complete. So far as I could determine, no one was rejected during this phase.

The next step was the swearing-in ceremony and the quick collecting of our draft classification cards. With that over with, we were bussed back to the dorm and told to get our gear for a trip to the train station. Train tickets and meal tickets were handed out and we were taken to the train.

It was evening when the train pulled out of Union Station. We settled into our Pullman berths and waited for a call to dinner. For most of us it was probably the first time that we had ridden a train in a sleeping car. We were called to the dining car for the last serving. Since we all had meal tickets, there was little choice to be made, and the service was not the best as there was little hope for a waiter's tip from among these enlistees. After dinner there were a few card games, but for the most part the men had their berths made up early. Many like me were reliving the events of the day and thinking of home while the clackity-clack of the rails made an attempt to lull them to sleep.

Day Two

This day was a blur of towns and countryside, of eating and talking, of new faces and old jokes, of card playing and napping, but it was not memorable in any way. No friends were made or even any names remembered. It was a fleeting relationship that was to mark nearly all encounters in the military for me. It was noted that our train had very low priority with regard to all other rail traffic. Every freight train and switch engine had priority over our movement. It would have been a lot faster trip by bus.

Day Three

We were all roused out of our berths and our sleep by the calls of the porter, "Everybody up; San Antonio." It was a little after four in the morning. We left the train bleary eyed to the shout of someone in uniform yelling, "Move it! Move it!" We trekked from the train to the waiting six by six, open trucks, where we boarded and rode like cattle the several miles from the San Antonio train station to Lackland Air Force Base, the Air Force Indoctrination Center.

We were unloaded at a mess hall and I noted that now our group had grown. Others from all parts of the United States were arriving as well. My group of new arrivals seemed to be the only ones who were eating breakfast. There were others in uniform beginning to trickle in by the time we had finished. I thought secretly that this may be some preplanned scheduling arrangement so that the older trainees would not be contaminated by us or would not see the multicolored clothing and the individual haircuts and go over the wall. Conversely, we might see the haircuts and the regimentation and make for the wall ourselves.

As we finished our first truly military meal, we were told to grab our gear and line up outside. This was to be our first "march," if you could call it that. The person in charge called out a cadence and directed us left and right, but that was the only resemblance to marching.

Our destination was the "Fun House." This "fun" part of the designation was certainly an exaggeration. This was where the serious changes began to be made toward turning one from a civilian into a GI. The first stop in this sprawling building was the barber shop. It was here that an equalization process was begun. Everyone received the same kind of haircut. The style embodied two major characteristics - off and bad. This was the first of the many assembly line procedures which we were to experience. The next stop was another physical examination, less thorough than the one at the induction center, but a bit tedious nonetheless. This was followed by a series of vaccination shots. As the second guy in front of me received a shot in each arm he fell face forward like a tree. He smashed his face into the concrete floor and broke out two of his front teeth. They carted him off to a nearby recovery room as if this was an everyday occurrence. As I went through the line, I heard comments from the staff on duty that this happened all the time. Why they did not take precautions against this, I was never able to find out.

After we had received our shots and got dressed, we were herded into a large holding area. Names were called out, and we were separated into groups. I found that these groups of 48 to 50 Airmen were "Flights," which made up "Squadrons," which were components of "Groups," which in turn were elements of a "Wing." Lackland Air Force Base was host to a training wing of the Air Training Command.

After all of these flights were formed, a very sharply dressed sergeant came in front our flight and announced that he was our "Flight Sergeant." This translated to tactical instructor, better known as a Drill Sergeant. He introduced two other men as assistant drill instructors, and then proceeded to disappear. The assistants then took charge of us and moved us to the next location.

The last stop in the Fun House was a warehouse-looking annex where we picked up our uniforms and other gear. We were one of the first groups coming through which were to receive the new Air Force blue uniform. Heretofore, the supplies had been limited, and the old Army olive drab had been issued. About the only article of clothing with which the duty attendants were the most concerned about fit, was the brogans. These high topped work shoes were not very pretty, but they were important to us. It was later that we learned to turn them into a thing of beauty with a lot of spit and polish, and a greater amount of elbow grease.

With loaded duffle bags, and still carrying all our civilian bags, we were herded (still not marching, though a half-hearted attempt was made) to our barracks. The trek was exhausting. It was well over a mile and the duffle was weighing an additional ten pounds with every block. At last we arrived at the ugly tar paper shack that was to be our home for the next eight weeks.

We were allowed about five minutes to collapse on the floor panting before we were called out again to line up and march to the "Supply Room" for bedding and additional equipment, such as mess kits, canteens, web belts, and other field gear. We returned to the barracks, stowed the supplies, and lined up for the evening meal. This was early for dinner, but our flight had missed lunch. We still looked miserable as we made our way toward the area mess hall. The term applied to all new troops not yet in uniform was "rainbows." This was taken from the various colors of the civilian clothing that everyone still wore.

As we made our way back to the barracks after the meal, there was a realization that something was happening to our gait, step, or pace. We were sounding a little more in sync in spite of ourselves. Perhaps the cadence being called by the assistant flight chief was beginning to sink in.

The first item of business was assigning bunks, and moving our footlockers and gear to the bunk location. The first thing that we were taught was how to roll our clothing and display our belongings in our footlockers. We had to lay out our personal toilet articles to start, but these were to be replaced with standard articles from the BX (Base Exchange) tomorrow.

We were given a short indoctrination about lights-out procedures, why to shake our brogans in the morning before putting them on (scorpions), and other minor housekeeping items, such as the danger of splinters from the rough wooden floor. The barracks were small tar paper shacks with no insulation and no foundation. They had been thrown together quickly for WWII, and had fallen into disuse. However, they were now serving to handle the overflow of personnel due to the buildup for the Korean conflict.

The remainder of the evening was devoted to making beds and learning how to wear our uniforms. "Hospital corners" was an arcane term to most of us as we learned how to fold, tuck and stretch the bedding until it was tight enough for the eagle eye of the instructors. One or two ritual sidelights came about during the evening. The first was the passing along a box into which we were to put all magazines, stories, dirty jokes, condoms, and nude pictures. We were to keep only one picture of our mother, wife or girlfriend. I often wondered what the confrontation would have been if the allowed picture had been a proscribed picture, i.e. nude. I later found that this raid upon our possessions was not to keep us pure so much as it was to provide several evening's worth of entertainment for the instructors, as they passed the juiciest items of the material from hand to hand.

The next ritual activity was the statement that we could send all of our civilian clothes home, or we could donate it to a worthy cause. The distance to the post office, lack of transportation, the cost of postage, and other inconveniences were cited by the instructors to help us all make up our minds that it would be easier to simply "donate" the clothing. There were some among us who had worn suits and expensive sports clothing. It was therefore rather disconcerting to see some of the Flight Chiefs throughout various units wearing our clothing in the months to come. The "worthy cause" was worthy only in the eye of the guy who was sporting our new threads.

And so to bed. We made the evening trek to the area latrine and hit the sack when the lights-out bugle call was broadcast all over the base by the loud speaker system. As I was reviewing the day in my mind before dropping off, I heard sobs from more than one area of the barracks. I could only guess that the day's stress had gotten to a few. It was either loneliness, anxiety, frustration, exhaustion, or any combination of those which could have affected the men emotionally. Nearly all of them were much younger than I. In fact, there were only two airmen who were older. These two were prior servicemen. There were three men who were enlisted with the rank of Private First Class, with one stripe already authorized. Two of these were the prior service men. The other had "earned his stripes" in the Civil Air Patrol. This made me angry. As a member of the Civil Air Patrol at home, no one ever mentioned to me that service credit could be earned.

Day Four

Reveille piped through the loud speakers brought us awake, and we staggered around trying to make beds, trying to get to the area latrine for showers and back, and trying to get into the unfamiliar clothing. We were ordered to line up for a march to the mess hall in much too quick a time for most of us. We went through the ordeal of standing at parade rest, coming to rigid attention, moving up in the line a few steps, then repeating the process for what seemed like blocks, as the queue snaked its way up to the serving line in the mess hall. Hunger had given way to criticism on the part of some of the new recruits. A few were complaining about the type and the taste of the food. I, for one, kept my mouth shut. I hadn't had it so good since I had left home more than five years before.

The morning was spent in learning our left foot from our right and how to make halfway decent movements while marching. A "Right Guide" was selected. This was an airman whose length of step and timing approached that of the ideal 30 inches and 120 steps per minute. He was the person who we all lined up with and with whom we were to keep in step while marching. A young black boy "with a sense of rhythm" got the job initially.

After another trip to the mess hall for the noon meal, we were marched to the paymaster for our first pay. This was to be sort of an advance for those of us who needed funds for any essentials during the coming weeks. We lined up in alphabetical order for what was to be the first of many of these kinds of formations for years to come. We drew our $60 in cash. A few of us felt rich beyond our wildest dreams, but only those poor slobs like myself who had seldom rubbed together more than fifty dollars at a time in our lives.

The next march was to the Base Exchange, where we were able to "exchange" some of the precious money we had just received, for towels, toilet articles, shoe polish, sewing kits and other sundries. We marched our purchases back to the barracks and spent the rest of the afternoon on the drill field sharpening our new skills in marching. After the evening meal, there was a mandatory period for writing letters home and instruction in how to wear the insignia we had purchased at the BX that afternoon. We were also taught how to shine our brogans and how to bleach our fatigue uniform so that it would not look so green and new. We made a fast, late evening march to the laundry with our khaki shirts and pants for altering, laundry, and starching with military creases. Then it was back to the barracks for more training.

In later weeks training often consisted of the Flight Chief putting a butt can in the middle of the floor and stating, "Do we have a GI party or do I go to town." The GI party meant that we were to scrub the rough wooden floor. The alternative was that we contribute to the butt can enough money to finance the DI's trip to town.

Along with all of this training came instruction in how to arrange our toiletries and clothing in our footlockers for the ever-present inspections that would soon be with us. We learned how to roll nearly every piece of clothing, shorts, socks, undershirts, towels, etc. so that they could be lined up on display. They had to be rolled tight enough so that rough handling would not cause the article to come unrolled. This was in the same category as tossing a quarter on the bunk to see if it was made up tight enough. If the quarter bounced, it was satisfactory.

Days Five Through Fifty

After the first few days of learning our left feet from our right feet, the training became pretty routine. Having had some close order drill experience in the Civil Air Patrol and some practice in drill and marching in my high school gym class, the marching routines were a snap. It was not long before I was promoted to "Right Guide" position and became the pivot person of the formation as well as carrying the honor flag of the unit. We lost the flight competition because some clown moved in ranks during a crucial formation, but we took second place because of our marching ability.

The never-ending academic classes in military customs and courtesy, first aid, military justice, chemical warfare, and other like subjects, all ran together. The droning of the not-too-experienced enlisted men doing the training put one to sleep very easily. Especially if you were tired from marching or it was afternoon after lunch. One "cure" for sleeping was being forced to hold your empty canteen over the edge of your desk. If you fell asleep, you then dropped the canteen to the floor with the attendant clatter and the subsequent embarrassment. I don't know how many times I dropped my canteen, but I finally was able to keep my eyes open by day dreaming, instead of listening to the low, monotonous tone of the lectures.

After the first month of training we were allowed a week-end pass to go to San Antonio. The first place I headed was the Alamo. I had heard so much about it, and had seen many movies in which it played a major role. I was very disappointed. It was just a dirty looking little building; not very impressive to be a famous landmark. Another item that was supposed to be major attraction was the San Antonio River. As far as I was concerned, it was an open sewer. Some of the bars along the river threw their garbage out the back door into the river, and I felt that some of the toilets drained into it as well. On one stretch of the river, they had canoe rentals where the tourists and trainees on an outing could take a canoe ride for want of something better to do. I took a pass on the canoe rides. I didn't want to fall into that stinking river. I had seen dead rats floating in it. Some of the guys did fall in. Their clothes dried fast enough, but the smell certainly did not go away. To jump ahead many years, they turned that open sewer into *El Paseo Del Rio*, and it is now a key sight to visit in San Antonio.

Company Punishment

After one particularly grueling morning on some sort of fatigue detail, and a late lunch, I found myself alone in the barracks one early afternoon. I thought to myself that I would just sit down to rest for a minute on the edge of my bed. In a moment, I said to myself, "I will just lie down for a second or two." The next thing I thought was that I would just close my eyes for a second. I then said to myself, "What is that thing smacking me in the face?" I opened my eyes to find a Lieutenant slapping me across the face with my hat, trying to wake me up.

The result of this little "rest" was the only disciplinary action taken against me during my entire military career. This "company punishment" consisted of wiping all the vending machines in the company area twice daily for two weeks. The labor was nothing, but the humiliation was most severe. My dereliction of duty, quitting my post, disobeying standing orders, and other crimes too numerous to mention, were all tied up in one little incident. I remember feeling at the time that I was lucky not to have been sent to Leavenworth, the way that they carried on.

Where to Go, What to Do?

As the time for technical school assignments drew near, I found that there were few opportunities for getting one's choice of school. There were lots of openings in the Air Police and for cooks and baker's school, but neither one of those appealed to me, especially since both schools were located in Biloxi, Mississippi, which was a hot and sticky climate, as well as a poor location for things to see and do. Radio and electronics schools interested me, but there was a limited availability for enrollment in those. In any case, it was believed by most of us that whatever you applied for there was someone who deliberately sent you somewhere else, in the perverse belief that it made you more ready for the change and the rigors of the military.

CHAPTER SEVEN:
PERMANENT PARTY

SINCE I HAD no desire to leave my fate to the whim of some unknown clerk, I decided to apply for permanent party and for the position of Drill Instructor (AKA Flight Chief, Drill Sergeant, or Tactical Instructor). The first step in applying for this job was to be interviewed by the Squadron Commander. The one "test" he gave me was to ask that I give a few commands. A requirement of the job was that the recruits could hear you across the parade ground. I was able to bellow loud enough for the light fixture to ring above the commander's desk.

He admitted later that he had not been too impressed with me until I had given the commands. After all, I did not fit the usual picture of a drill sergeant. I was only about five-eight in height, wore glasses, and was not otherwise big enough to frighten anyone who might want to sit on me. Part of the role of the DI was to intimidate to obtain compliance, where leadership might fail.

With regard to a command voice, it was the practice of the Flight Chiefs to sit lazily on the steps of their barracks and drill the troops up and down the street, often nearly a block away. In parades, voice commands had to carry a great distance because the numbers of troops in one marching unit could be more than a hundred (12 x 12), and the position of the one calling the commands was some distance away.

With the Commander's endorsement for permanent party locked up, I now knew what I would be doing. This knowledge of where I was going and what I would be doing was worth any number of prestige points, *vis-à-vis* my fellow Airmen. I could sit back and relax while they sweated out their worldwide assignments. Many had their hearts set on immediately going to Korea, knowing that there would be little front line activity for an Airman. Others wanted a technical school first before going.

Basic training was now over at Lackland, and I was free of the stifling regimentation and make-work projects that typified most of our activities. The graduation ceremony was just another boring parade as far as I was concerned. We had had one of those each Saturday since I had been here.

Most of the new graduates got busy sewing on their first stripe after the graduation ceremony. I was going to get to sew two stripes on my sleeves. The Flight Commanders, of which I was going to be one, got to wear corporal stripes. The rank was only "acting," but it separated us from the rabble. The real separation from the mass of personnel was the fact that I was now "permanent party," or part of the regular base cadre making up the operation of the base mission, that of training newly enlisted personnel.

Most everyone was elated to be graduated, but it seemed that most were more elated simply to be on their way to something new. I, however, had no such change to look forward to. I was now relegated to repeating basic training again and again. The only difference was that I was not going to be in the formation while doing it, and I would be calling the cadence, instead of marching to it.

A Fast Trip Home

The squadron spent a week or two indoctrinating the few of us new drill instructors. They taught us how to be "a leader of men." Part of the free time we had, I used to scrub my fatigue uniforms many times and bleach and starch them. The idea was to look "saltier" than I really was to the new recruits that I would be picking up soon. With weekends now free, I was able to take a quick trip home to see Mom and Dad. I got a ride with someone from the base that lived in Kansas, not far from home. It was a long and frantic weekend trip. I stayed at home only one night before I had to go back. I don't remember any names, places, or faces about that trip. In retrospect, it was dumb trip, but I thought that I would not get to see Mother and Dad for some time after I started to take trainees through the program. Once home, I kept them awake far into the night regaling them about my "adventures" in the Air Force. I had not been very good about writing since I had left in early October. This was now late November and I nothing much had changed at home.

Mexico, Ole!

On our next available free weekend, several of us loaded up for a trip to Mexico. I was looking forward to seeing a foreign, exotic country. Instead, I found it to be a dirty, smelly place of easy women, cheap food, and cheaper booze. I remember we all had huge steaks in this big restaurant, and washed them down with water glasses full of Zombies. We were all "feeling no pain." We managed to get back to our car, where we slept off the booze the rest of the afternoon.

We awoke from our "nap" just in time for the night life to start. The kids, to whom we had given a few pesos to watch the car, had literally ground the paint off of it by wiping the dust from it with dry rags. The sandy dust served as a good paint remover to take much of the finish off the car.

The fact that Laredo was a border town was the reason that Mexico did not leave a very good taste in my mouth. The curio shops with their shoddy merchandise, everyone tugging at your sleeve to buy something, and every dirty urchin that I ran across seeming to have a "sister" that he wanted me to meet, did not give me much of a reason to want to return again soon.

One thing we did that will stick in my mind was that we went to a bull fight. In spite of the fact that it was a small bull ring, and the Toreadors fighting were not noted, the pomp and the ceremony were very colorful. The thing that struck me as unusual about the bull fight, other than the fight itself and the slaying of the bull, was that everywhere you looked, especially walking along the upper rim of the stadium, were many uniformed national police carrying big machine guns. It looked like they were prepared for a huge riot or a small war.

My First Recruits

The following week after my trip to Mexico I was notified that I was to get my first flight of new recruits. I picked up these troops and started basic all over again. With the recent memory of my basic training fresh in my mind, I made up my mind that I would not make the same mistakes my drill instructor had made, and that I would treat the recruits as human beings, instead of like dogs. Well, circumstances quickly made me forget to be nice and I was soon a Mad Dog Tactical Instructor just like the rest of them. The press of time did not allow for niceties.

The influx of new trainees was taxing the ability of the base to handle them. The Korean conflict had generated a surge of volunteers for the Air Force. The new enlistees were probably here as a way to avoid the draft and mandatory service in the Army than any great altruistic call to defend a way of life.

Tents were being erected on every parade ground and every other available space. Mess halls were in operation 24 hours a day and other facilities supporting the training mission were at the limit of their capabilities.

It was at this time that we heard that a new training base was opening. Headquarters put out a call for volunteers to serve as the first permanent cadre to man the new base. I had not yet been successful in finding a technical school which interested me enough to apply, and those persons going overseas were still cooks and Air Police. One often-mentioned enticement as a reason to apply for the new assignment was that there would probably be a wide open opportunity for advancement in rank and a good choice of positions at this new installation. Since I was always on the alert for something new and different, I put my name on the list.

It was not long before I heard a reply. I was on orders to go before I knew what was happening. I would not even get to see my first flight of new recruits through until their graduation. I was soon relieved from my drill instructor duties to out-process and to make arrangements for a long delay in route home for Christmas.

Reassignment and Home For Christmas

I could not believe that I had been so lucky as to be home for Christmas. The reassignment was starting off with good omens of things to come. Little did I know. At home, Mother and I were finally able to clear my room at Fasts. These were the last few remnants of my nearly seven years of living there. We had a nice Christmas with everyone home for the holidays. It wasn't all that noteworthy perhaps, but it was certainly a relaxing time for me after the several months of hectic activity. One embarrassing note was that Mother, in her pride for her "little boy," had tinted my basic training graduation picture and had hung it on the wall. That ruddy faced little cherub was not the vision I had of myself as the steely eyed Drill Master.

When it came time for me to leave, my parents took me to the train. I remember that the train was so full of servicemen home for the holidays, that the club car was full, the dining car was full and people were standing in the aisles and in the vestibules. Those in the dining car were seated, and were sleeping with their heads on the tables. The crowd on the train thinned out when I changed trains in Chicago, but there was still a press of people.

My first look at Chicago filled this country boy with awe and wonder. As I walked slowly across the Loop I saw sights that this kid from the flat lands had never seen before. I took time out to see Minsky's Burlesque. To me, Minsky's was one of the "seven wonders of the world" with all those scantily clad beauties parading about.

I wondered at the tall buildings, and marveled at the hustle and bustle that had not been prevalent in Kansas City. As I made my way around the Loop, I was approached by many lovely ladies of the evening. Little did they know that my pockets held little more than lint.

As I boarded the train for the continuation of my journey to New York, I was captivated by the sonorous calls of the train destination announcements. The reverberations of the sound in that huge station, and the strange sounding names of the cities sent cold shivers up and down my spine. I can still remember some of the stations announced for that Chicago to New York City trip on the New York Central Railroad, ". . . Gary, Erie, Ashtabula, Toledo, Buffalo."

CHAPTER EIGHT:
SAMPSON AFB

SAMPSON AIR FORCE Base was named for Admiral William T. Sampson, a naval hero of the past. This facility had been a Navy training base during World War II. It was directly on the eastern shore of Lake Seneca, a very deep lake, the largest of the Finger Lakes, in upstate New York. The Navy had abandoned the facility after the war, and it had been alternately used as an agricultural college and a grain storage site. The buildings had largely fallen into disrepair, especially with regards to heating and plumbing. The Air Force had accepted the base from the Navy in 1950, during the Korean War. It later closed in 1956 when the Air Force enlistments declined dramatically.

The Navy had walked away from the base without any attempt to clean or preserve it. There were remains of quarters of beef still hanging in what had been the meat lockers. There was bread still in the bread mixers at the bakery and the switches were still covered with dough. It was as if a doughy hand had turned off the switches and the owner walked away. The thirteen or fourteen years since the Navy left had not been good for the base. In addition to the weather and time taking their tolls, many windows had been the target of vandals.

When I arrived, it was the first week of January. I could not believe how bleak it was. Nothing had prepared me for what appeared to be conditions as bad as the front lines of Korea. The barracks to which I was assigned had no heat, no hot water, and no bedding. We had to go to bed with our clothes on. We slept on the floor on thin straw mattresses left over by the Navy and we would pull one or two of these over us for warmth. There was no water to drink except in the mess hall where we could get coffee, or we could go to one of the few buildings on the base with heat and get bottles of soda out of the vending machines. They would not put vending machines in the barracks, because the bottles would freeze and burst.

Since there were no new trainees to perform the usual house-keeping and maintenance duties, the recently assigned permanent party did all the dirty details. Most of us had to perform these details in our dress uniforms, because our work gear had not been shipped by the Air Force from Lackland AFB. Many of us had to work for weeks in the same dress uniform. I would take a bus to Geneva, New York, about once a week and rent a room in a hotel. Here I would take a shower and wash clothes in the sink.

Geneva was not a very hospitable place for servicemen. They still had a bad taste in their mouth from the memory of the Navy being nearby. Geneva was purported to be the original location of the sign, "Sailors and Dogs Keep Off the Grass." I guess the boys in navy blue had despoiled all their women and drunk all of their booze (and booze had been hard to get during the war).

The weather was also very inhospitable. It seemed that the roads were always a glare of ice from the frozen spray from the lake where the road hugged the lake shore. Many of the new permanent party did not know how to drive in icy weather conditions, and a lot of our people were lost to vehicle accidents.

I Pick Up Another Flight

I was assigned to pick up one of the first new Basic flights to take them through basic training. I remember one big, pale faced Jewish boy came up to me with a big box. His mother had baked a cake for him to take to his "leader," and he had protected it from damage all the way from New York City while juggling his bags and moving from bus, to train, to bus, and so on. He tried to give it to me, but I had to refuse. I could not be in a position to accept anything from anyone. In the event that he became a sharp Airman, it would have been "because of the gift." I forced him to give it to the men in the supply lines before we left the building. He was very disheartened.

I had to drill these basic trainees for several weeks in the clothing they brought with them, augmented by very moldy WWII surplus overcoats. When it rained, a barracks full of stinking, wet, moldy wool was something else. It was their civilian shoes that were the worst problem. These troops had to march in cold, wet weather, in shoes that were ill-suited to the task.

Why the Air Force had decided to reopen this facility as a basic training center no one would ever know. The weather was not very agreeable except in late spring and early fall. The cold wind and freezing rain blowing off Lake Seneca presented a forbidding environment to half-dressed recruits drilling in the open air. They were half-dressed because logistics had not caught up with the other parts of the plan. Uniforms and other essential items, such as bedding had not been shipped to anticipate the new troop arrivals. When clothing did arrive, it was diverted World War II Army uniforms - olive drab wool and brown leather. The new Air Force blue uniforms were being issued at Lackland, and had been for several months.

One incident that sticks in my mind somewhat typifies the fear and intimidation that is imparted by drill instructors to new recruits in an unfamiliar setting. One of the first evenings I was giving the "fear of God" to the recruits, wherein I inspected them while they stood a rigid attention. If there was anything wrong with their dress, posture, or their display, I would get in their face and promise them the end of the world if they did not shape up. This one recruit was receiving a particularly salty version of my wrath, when he lost control of his bladder in front of me. I suddenly realized, more than I ever had before, the power of life and death I had over these little mounds of clay. It made me realize that I had a big responsibility here, that of turning these kids into men.

I took only one flight completely through basic training before I was promoted to Buck Sergeant and assigned as a Tactical NCO. This meant I was to supervise several tactical instructors, while I secretly harbored the insecurity that I was not yet a seasoned tactical instructor myself. While my career as a Drill Sergeant was short lived, I used that experience to good advantage in many war stories with "Old Salts" in later years.

After a time as Tactical NCO, I was offered the opportunity to serve as an instructor for a new rehabilitation experiment that was being tried in the Air Police unit. Instead of serving their time in the stockade certain prisoners were, after much screening, allowed to continue with certain kinds of military instruction, to include a generous amount of military Courtesy and Discipline training. This was to enable them to become more productive Airmen once their sentences were up.

I was never able to really check on the recidivism rate of these people.

I don't know whether the training did any good to prevent having repeat offenders or not. This was an experiment for which no test results were available.

Prisoner Chasing

One of the opportunities of which I was able to take advantage while I was assigned to this unit was serving as a "prison chaser." When an Airman went AWOL, and was later captured or turned himself in, someone had to go after him. To use the experienced Air Police for this duty was a waste of manpower, so the duty usually went to someone who was not in an essential position, or as a reward for doing something exceptional. Since my job was nonessential, and I was able to hear of the returns first, I was able to go after many prisoners across the U.S.

We always travelled in pairs by train and were given meal tickets for food for ourselves and the prisoner. We would use up our own meal tickets, and we then used the prisoner's meal tickets for sandwiches, which we would then divide among the three of us. We were admonished never to handcuff a prisoner to a stationary object. We always rationalized that the seat of the train was not stationary. After all, it was moving down the track, so we would handcuff the prisoner to a seat and spend most of the trip back in the club car. We had few incidents. One prisoner tried to break out the window of the train washroom while we were moving down the track, one tried to escape the day we arrived and was shot in the leg climbing a fence, and one went back to his cell and cut his wrists when he heard we had come for him. We took him anyway.

Whenever we passed through Chicago we were very glad. They had a military holding facility at Union Station where we could check our prisoner. They would house and feed him until we picked him up again. We could also leave our pistols there. However, some of the guys wanted to wear theirs all the time, because it looked cool. That lasted until some prison chaser got drunk while wearing his weapon and shot up Union Station. After that we could only wear our weapon when we had a prisoner in custody. It was always nice to spend a few days in Chicago. There was always something to do. I especially remember the big USO club they had on Michigan Avenue. There was always good food, soft drinks, a bed to sleep in if you were tired, and a nice girl to dance with in the evenings.

Extracurricular Activities

One summer an inquiry was made if there was anyone who would be willing to work evenings at a laundry in Geneva. They did uniforms as their main business. They could not find many locals to do the job, so they opened it up to base personnel. I wanted to pick up some spending money so I took one of the available jobs. I was now sending money home to my parents to help out. The job paid well, but it was like working in a steam bath. The hot weather, plus the steam of the pressing machines was torture at times. I certainly ironed a lot of shirts while it lasted. When the cool weather returned at last, along with the regular employees, I was out of a job. However, I can't say that I was too disappointed.

With what now seemed a lot of time on my hands, since I was no longer working, I enrolled in several AFIT courses. One of these was a German language course. I got good grades, but since there were no opportunities to practice the language and no good reason to remember it, any knowledge of it soon went away. I also tried my hand at fencing. I went to the extent of buying an expensive saber, a fencing mask, and a canvas vest. I took saber lessons for several months from an Olympic champion who was assigned to special services on the base. I was still taking fencing lessons when I was reassigned. I thought I got quite good at the sport, but I never again could find anyone to practice with, so I finally sold my saber, mask, and other gear years later.

One of the projects for which I volunteered, was as a member of the Sampson AFB ceremonial drill team. We were outfitted with chrome helmets, white belts, white aiguillettes, and white boot laces. We carried M1 rifles. The braided aiguillette accessory looked very cool on the blue uniforms. We were quite good and were invited to many of the local parades and ceremonies throughout Central New York.

After the start of a sequence we could perform for several minutes without another command. One of our routines was to remove our helmets and merge into the crowd. The Drill Master would walk to the middle of the street in front of the reviewing stand and blow a whistle. We would appear from all directions, hit the formation in seconds, and begin our act, almost before the crowd knew what had happened. At the end of our routine, we would not simply march away, but would disappear into the crowd in the same way that we came in.

When there was no reviewing stand and the crowds were not in one location, we would end up marching a parade route doing our trick formations along the way, often ending up in the middle of some local football field where we did our routines for the crowd.

Another activity, in which I volunteered to serve, was to help control civilian traffic at the big International Sports Car Race, The Grand Prix, at Watkins Glen. The few of us who volunteered for this duty got to see the races, and the other associated activities, up close and involved. With official badges and uniforms we were given the run of the race course, the pits, and the refreshment stands. Watkins Glen was a picturesque town located in rolling hills at the lower end of Lake Seneca. The torturous, winding roads, and the fast up and downhill race course, gave quite a test of skills to the drivers, who came from around the world for this event.

Other than for the race, the area was noted for vineyards, and Penn Yann, a women's teachers college. The thrill of the races was great. The thrill of trying to score at an all girls' school was also great. However, the thrill of the chase was only that, the chase and nothing more. I was able to participate two years in a row in the Grand Prix duty. The second year did not quite have the excitement and newness of the first, but it was great fun.

As I mentioned earlier, Geneva was not a very good liberty town. Most everyone went to Syracuse, Rochester, Buffalo, or surrounding smaller towns for entertainment. I gravitated to Rochester for reason that transportation was more convenient for me, since I had no car. There was a bus station on the base and there was a direct bus from the base to Rochester, with several busses during the day and night, both going and returning. Rochester was big enough to absorb the servicemen who might wish to go there without it appearing to be a military town.

Rochester was the home of Kodak, and was noted for its Lilacs. It also had some wide open bars, the most notable of which was the Glass Bar and Machine Gun Kellys. The first bar had a nice dance band, but it also had a very nice strip show on the bar on Friday and Saturday nights. I, of course, went for the drinks. They served a very tasty Singapore Sling, which happened to be my sissy drink of the season.

When I was not in Rochester, I was usually out with my roommate at a local bar (five miles from the base). He was the squadron Chief Clerk. He handled assignments and records for the basic trainees as well as for permanent party. Once we drew a trip together to go after a prisoner, and I stayed with his folks in Indianapolis a night on our way through.

He always drank too much and we would often close a bar, and weave from one side of the road to the other while driving back. He would never let me drive; always insisting that he was sober enough to handle it. One evening he asked me to go with him, but I begged off because I had some letters to write. That night as he returned, he turned at what he thought was the entrance to the base, but it was two hundred yards too soon. Going approximately eighty miles an hour, he hit a tree and was killed instantly. I'm certainly glad for those letters I had to write (or fate).

Out of the blue one day, I received orders reassigning me to another base. I was not too unhappy about changing jobs, but I did not want to lose my current girlfriend. It was so very hard for me to establish new relationships that I did not wish to go through that agony and frustration all over again, elsewhere.

Many of the first cadres to arrive on the base were receiving orders to go overseas or to other bases. I really don't know why the military must decide that people have to move after a given time in a job. It certainly does not provide for continuity of information, nor the development of skills to their optimum. In twenty years I was never able to really find out. With but little fanfare at the base, and a teary farewell to the girlfriend, I was on my way again.

CHAPTER NINE:
F. E. WARREN AFB

FRANCIS E. WARREN Air Force Base, Wyoming was a base of the Air Training Command. It was now the home of several technical schools to include several levels of supply school, cryptography school, and several kinds of clerical and personnel schools. The schools' side of the base was temporary barracks and classrooms, made of wood framing with tar paper roofs. They were built for Army training during World War II. The permanent side of the base was old, solid brick structures dating back to the days when it was Fort D.A. Russell, a cavalry post. In fact, some offices were now located in what had once been stables. An apocryphal story was that a valid set of orders for the installation still remained in effect, to wit: "There shall be no shooting of bison from the second story windows."

The Assignment

My new assignment was to the 3462nd Student Squadron as a Training NCO. The mission of the squadron was to house, pay, and otherwise tend to the needs of the students while they attended a supply school. Other student squadrons had similar missions to serve the other technical schools located on the base.

My job was to drill the troops, march them to their school, teach military subjects in the squadron, inspect their barracks, arrange for supply formations, and otherwise baby sit them while they attended technical school. There were four of us training NCOs to do a job that the First Sergeant could have done in his spare time. Looking back, I can't possibly remember what I did that would have kept me busy enough to deserve being paid.

My Caddy

The bar scene soon got old, and since it had been four years that I had been without wheels, I decided go to work nights for a little extra money for a car of some sort. I got a job at a small snack bar next to the squadron, bussing tables, acting as short order cook, washing dishes, and whatever else they might assign. I then got a job as bartender at the NCO Club. The pay was not that much better, but the tips were great. However, I had to perform some fakery to collect.

After I had put a little money ahead, and while home on my next leave, I began to look seriously for a car. I was not intending to buy anything quite so expensive, but I saw a 1953 Coupe d'Ville Cadillac in the showroom and I had to have it. It was jet black with a cream top and tons of chrome.

Mother and Dad shook their heads, but Dad co-signed the note for me to finance it. I was soon on my way back to Wyoming in style. That "style" kept me broke for a long time while I paid for it, but I came out way ahead in the end.

I was now able to come home more often. It was over 600 miles home from the base, however, I could made it with only a few stops for gas. The Cadillac would get over 22 miles per gallon, and it was only my bladder which caused me to stop more often than the gas tank did. I often got very sleepy on those long trips, though. With the things that I had to do to keep awake it's a wonder that I'm still here to write about it.

I remember one amusing incident with the car, which at the time was terror ridden. The Caddy was equipped with an Autronic Eye, which was to dim the lights when another car approached. I was driving my usual "Kansas speed limit" when I met a car, and as they were supposed to do, the headlights dimmed for the approaching vehicle. So far so good. The car passed, but instead of the lights changing back bright they went out. Here I am, at eighty miles plus per hour, tearing down a curving road with no lights in the dead of night. I quickly stomped and stomped for the foot button which served as an override switch.

The lights finally came on as I was moving into a sharp curve to the right. I had been concentrating so much on finding the foot switch that I had not hit the brakes. The only bright spot was that repairs only cost ninety-five cents for a fuse in the "eye." They could have charged me much more and I wouldn't have known the difference.

I was now able to make an occasional trip to Denver without asking to go along with someone or waiting for an infrequent invitation. That long straight road to Denver was always very enticing to test the top speed of a big Cadillac. I was never ticketed, but was stopped once after having been followed for nearly fifty miles at over eighty miles per hour. After finally stopping me, the patrolman reminded me that, "We have a speed limit in Colorado." I was displaying Kansas plates, and the speed limit in Kansas was "safe and reasonable," whatever that meant. He let me go without a ticket, and to this day I can't figure out why.

Frontier Days

No mention of Francis E. Warren Air Force Base, and its neighboring city, Cheyenne, the capital city of Wyoming, is complete without mentioning Frontier Days. This is a week for rodeo lovers from everywhere, and when everyone dresses Western. The Frontier Days Celebration is held annually in July. The first one was held in 1897.

Cheyenne was a wide open town during those years. It was the home of "The Daddy of Them All," Frontier Days Rodeo. During all times of the year, and not just for Frontier Days, everyone dressed the role. After all, this was an old "cow town" and there was a reputation to uphold. The deprecating remark often heard was, "Cowboy hats are like hemorrhoids, sooner or later every asshole has one." I could not escape either. I got the hat, boots and the tight western pants with the big buckle, "Whee, I was a cowboy!" At least I blended in with every other dude who went to town for a Tivoli beer. Those boots were the first ones I ever owned, despite having grown up part of my life on a ranch.

During Frontier Days, the days are spent in the big arena watching bucking horses, bull riding, calf roping, chuck wagon races, bulldogging, Indian war dances, and any number of other Western amusements. The nights are spent in revelry, in which it seemed to be illegal to appear sober. I watched, among other things, horses being ridden through the lobby and bar of one of the best hotels in town, and people camping the night in store alcoves, public parks, and the front yards of ordinary citizens. Beverage bottles and cans were as thick as drifted snow everywhere. It seemed as if all the cowboys and pretend cowboys from everywhere showed up for Frontier Days.

Most of the Airmen at the base who could manage a day off went to the celebration (both day and night activities). I, for one, joined the crowd. I went to the Rodeo portion of the Frontier Days Celebration one day, and bar hopping one night. The crowds were so thick that you could not walk into a bar with your hands at your sides because you could not bring them up to take a drink, let alone reach into your pocket to pay for it.

The second year I was stationed at the base, I had not planned to go downtown for Frontier Days, but my parents visited me, so I had to get seats for us at the arena for one day's Rodeo. The next day after that, I took them for a drive to some of the scenic sights in Colorado before they drove home. The big hoot for my father was when we crossed over the Continental Divide. He asked if he could stop. After that he was able to brag that he took a leak in both oceans at the same time.

I Sign Over

I had reached the end of my four year enlistment and was at the decision point of whether to reenlist or not. I had not yet made up my mind at the time that I signed my final papers for separation. I walked out of the building as a civilian, walked one complete circle of the block, came back in the door that I had just left, and reenlisted for six years. In that circle of the block I was forced to examine my options as I had not been forced to do previously. I had no real prospects for any kind of a job and certainly no real future. I could not see myself going back to Montgomery Ward or some other equally prosaic job. That walk around the block was probably the most propitious of my life, and certainly a greater turning point than when I first enlisted in the Air Force.

Not much really changed with my job. I went back to doing the same thing that I had been doing. They had not obtained a replacement for me. I still had to work to keep up car payments, but I was freer to travel around than I had been. I continued to work at the NCO club as a bartender. The problem was that instead of tipping you, the customer often would want to buy you a drink. You could not keep this up very long on a busy evening, so you prepared a special bottle of tea, or a mixture of Seven-Up and cola to look like whisky or scotch, poured your "drink" and rang up the sale. You collected the difference, keeping track of the drinks with a toothpick. After the evening was over, you collected from the cash drawer.

The women were always the toughest customers to wait on. They always dreamed up the fanciest drink they could think of, especially when some guy was paying for it. The most difficult drink for me to make was the "*Pousse-Café,*" (often called a Rainbow). Several layers of liquor must be poured on the back of a bar spoon so they would not mix, then it is topped with a layer of cream. It seemed that the bar was always busiest when one of these was ordered, and that other bartenders were always jostling my arm. The final blow would come when the drink was tossed off in one gulp, or it was mixed by the customer before drinking. The classic way to drink the drink is to sip it one layer at a time, savoring each taste as a complement to the bartender for keeping the tastes separate.

The other thing I remember about that job was the mistake jar. Any mistake we made while mixing, or a wrong order, we could dump into our own "mistake jar." Since it was saddening to be "wasting the booze," we would drink our mistakes after the bar closed. The guy with the clearest head in the morning had made the fewest mistakes with his drinks the night before.

During the time that I was stationed here, I joined the Masonic order. The Mess Sergeant was a Mason, and after I asked to join, he sponsored me and served as my tutor. I went through the first three degrees as fast as they offered them. At the next opportunity I applied for the Scottish Rite (32nd Degree). I was initiated into those 29 degrees at the 100th reunion of the Cheyenne Consistory. I have always been sorry that I have not been able to devote more time to the organization. They not only do good work, but their philosophy is a very selfless and altruistic one.

While I had been in good favor with most of my superiors during my tour at Francis E. Warren, I was especially pleased to be promoted to the position of First Sergeant of the Squadron. The position usually called for someone of more rank than I had on my sleeve, but the Commander had faith in my abilities and I did not let him down. The duties were not that difficult, and one of the perks that came with the job was the key to the Mess Hall. I was now able to fry steak and eggs when I came home late at night, and did so with some regularity.

In my new and responsible position as First Sergeant, I came into more frequent contact with the Squadron Commander, Captain Mitchell. I suppose he may have been impressed by my ambition or my knowledge, but whatever the reason, he often suggested that I apply for Officer Candidate School. He mentioned it to me more often as time passed, because he was aware, as was I, that I was fast approaching the time when I would no longer be eligible for reason of age.

I finally made the decision that I would give it a try. It was a big decision, so much so that it marked the end of another phase of my life. I considered calling the next part of my little narrative: "Part III, In Which I Become an Officer and a Gentleman, by Order of the President of the United States." However, that was a bit wordy, so I simply entitled it: "Military Life: The Middle Years."

PART III:
MILITARY LIFE: THE MIDDLE YEARS

THE RAREFIED ATMOSPHERE of the officer class did not appeal to me all that much, but I felt that I was dying on the vine in my then current position as an enlisted man. Even though I had received good breaks, and was now a First Sergeant, the long range opportunity for promotions was looking bleaker as the Korean War wound down. I wanted bigger challenges, so I decided to follow my CO's suggestion, and apply for Officer Candidate School.

I was encouraged by my commander, Captain Mitchell. He and his staff of officers gave me glowing written recommendations. I laid my plans carefully by taking as many of the AFIT (Air Force Institute of Technology) courses as I could. I also wrote to a State Senator in Kansas and asked him for a recommendation to the school. I gave a big line of bull about how my father was a rancher who had supported his candidacy in the past. That part of the plan paid off. I don't know how effective the letter was, but I later learned that my records had a "PI" notation for many years. That meant "political influence," which in some quarters was <u>not</u> a nice thing to have in your records.

My biggest preparation was the purchase of a pair of contact lenses. This meant several trips to Denver and a considerable cost outlay. Contact lenses were a new technology, and not every optometrist yet fitted people for them. I knew that to pass the vision test, I would have to be able to see even better than I did. When I was in high school, I had taken the Navy "V12" test to become an officer in the Navy. I went to Wichita and took the test, which lasted nearly all day. I passed the test with good grades, and was called to Kansas City to take the physical.

They took one look at my glasses and gave me a vision test. Since they could not provide me with guide dog service, they rejected me, then gave me hell for taking up their time. I was supposed to know that I should not have applied if I had bad vision.

To make a long story short, the preliminary physical which was to accompany the completed OCS application was passed with flying colors. I simply had to remember in what sequence to wear what glasses.

I filed my application and waited. That was about the longest three months of my life until I heard that I had been accepted. My relief and joy brought me about as close to tears as anything associated with the military had done in the past, or would ever do in the future. I was able to realize that this could mean a whole new way of life to me and could change my future considerably. Now, if I could only hold on to graduate.

CHAPTER TEN:
OFFICER CANDIDATE SCHOOL

ON MY WAY to OCS, I stopped at home for a delay in route. To this day I remember a picnic that Mom arranged, and the watermelon we had. It was the best watermelon I could ever remember eating. There is even photographic evidence of that event. I am standing with a piece of watermelon in my hand and watermelon all over my face. One other thing about that picture, it also reflects my first GI haircut that I had since I was in basic training. I had gotten a short haircut in anticipation of the haircut to come when I entered officer school.

My visit home came to an end, and I began my drive to Lackland AFB, Texas, and the school. Everything went well until I arrived at San Marcos, Texas. I was travelling down the highway minding my own business, when out of the blue, someone pulled out and smacked me in the left rear quarter of my shiny Cadillac. It was the first accident I had had with my car. The police gave the other driver a ticket for failing to yield, but the driver later tried to sue me for damages, injury to his daughter, and any number of other things. I guess he felt that since I was driving a big car and was in the military that I was ripe for picking. My insurance settled the case and repaired my car, but the situation was disruptive of my school, and having to explain the accident to superiors was no fun.

Welcome to Hell

Once having been billeted and supplied at the school, I found myself in a living hell. The hazing by the upper class, the grueling schedule, the tough grind of the academic work, and the constant testing of one's ability to "take it", both mentally and physically, really took me to the edge. Many fellow classmates were eliminated by the pressure. The hours of marching penalty "tours" on the ramp were nothing compared to the psychological torture. I made up my mind that if others had made it, I could too. My determination was all too often reflected in my face. If I became angry at the hazing, my face would become red as a beet and they would be quick to penalize me for "emoting." Since I was not able to vent my anger vocally or physically, I simply boiled inside and spent a lot of penalty tours marching on the ramp.

Most of my fellow classmates were married. This was the first time that I came to realize that a wife might be a nice thing to have. The wives were able to do laundry, starch and iron uniforms, sew on insignia, provide emergency food, run errands, and do any number of very necessary tasks that had to be done. This provided more time for the candidates to study, and to arrange their clothing and locker displays for inspections.

Passing inspections was a very vital aspect to the OCS regimen. To make a long story short, I failed to pass a lot of inspections and more than once I had to iron clothes in the dark, after lights were out. I remember one candidate, who was ironing in the dark, had mistakenly applied furniture polish to his uniform instead of liquid starch. He was not aware of the mistake until the light of day, when he had to put on the uniform and wear it to a formation.

Many small trials and tribulations abound, but one comes to mind. Keeping one's toiletries display pristine and always ready for inspection was a large task in itself. To gain some time and effort in this area everyone was always looking for a "program beater." In my case, I kept a razor for display, and carried another around in my pocket to use. I used hand soap for shaving cream and this dull razor until one morning I took a large gash out of my face while sharing the mirror with about twelve other guys. I could not stop the blood before it was time to stand up for roll call out on the parking ramp. That morning for inspection I must have looked a pretty sight with blood pouring down my face and onto my shirt. Needless to say, I received a penalty. The charge: Damage to government property ... Me.

Hazing tactics and dumb-seeming requirements were many. Toilet articles had to be displayed on a clean towel tight against the side of a drawer. If an item was tapped, and it clicked against the drawer, it "was not flush" and resulted in a gig (demerit). If you used a penny under the towel to prop the item against the side of the drawer so that it wouldn't click, and that penny was found, it was an "unauthorized object" and worth a gig. Upper classmen would come through the rooms while we were out and put bits of confetti in the pockets of uniforms hanging in the closets. If these tiny bits of colored paper were found at the time of inspection, they were "unauthorized objects" and worth a gig for each bit of paper one found.

We were required to memorize random bits of nonsense which had to be repeated when requested by an upper classman. The correct reply to, "Mister, give me a statement," was, "Sir, uga, ugaboo, ugaboo, boo, uga." The response to, "Mister, what time is it?" was (with your watch in front of your face), "Sir, although the inner workings and hidden mechanisms of my chronometer are not in accord with the great celestial magnitudes by which time is most commonly governed, I feel that I may say, without being court-martialed for perjury, that the time is approximately (give hour and minute) two ticks and a tock." The answer to, "What did Teddy Roosevelt say?" was, "Charge!" One catch-all phrase required for no particular reason: "Thirty days hath September, April, June, and no wonder. All the rest have peanut butter sandwiches, except Grandmother, and she rides a chartreuse motor scooter."

I was the second oldest candidate in my class, and some of the activities seemed pretty petty and childish to me. This did not seem to be a way to build leaders of men. It seemed better suited to teach a band of mindless followers, but what the hell, I had to put up with it. Rather that accepting the program, I only tolerated it. My attitude probably did much to make things harder for me. It was only when we were involved in purely academic pursuits that I really perked up.

The War Games

The field exercises of the program took place at Camp Bullis, Texas, a large, rambling military installation several miles from Lackland. We were armed with military weapons firing blanks, and we were formed into two teams, Red and Blue, with the typical exercises of capturing enemy territory, prisoners and equipment. It was pretty basic military tactics practice.

The final exercise of the war games was the Escape and Evasion problem. We were divided into teams of five and given a compass, taken out ten miles from the main camp, and dumped in the dark. Our mission was to make our way back to camp before dawn by making certain checkpoints and navigating our way home. Upper classmen were the opposing forces and were laying in ambush all over the area. There were very few teams that avoided capture. My team was successful, but I still carry a scar on my leg where I ran full speed into a barbed wire fence. I avoided capture, but I walked into camp with my boot full of blood. That gave me another scar to carry to my grave.

The flurry of activities as an upper classman was not very eventful or memorable. The second half of the program began immediately after the upper class graduated, I became part of the new upper class and a new class arrived. Our status had now been changed, and the hazees were now to be the hazers. We were now forced to do much the same thing to our lower class as was done to us. My heart was not in this anymore than it was when I was on the receiving end, so I avoided most of the hazing activities wherever possible.

One of the projects assigned to the upper class was that each squadron (of eight) had to write a war plan. The winning war plan would be used by the school in the war games field exercise which was a part of the training. I ended up writing the war plan for our squadron almost in its entirety. It was the winning plan for the school. For that honor I was promoted to operations officer for the war games and got to man all the communications and direct the war games from the command center.

During the upper class phase, there was more concentration upon academics, and I was able to make up some of the ground that I had lost earlier with regard to class standing. Class standing was based upon grades, fellow classmates' ratings, demerits, attitude, and any number of other evaluations. I had not done well as a lower classman.

I Become an Officer and a Gentleman

As graduation approached, assignments were being determined. I applied for Personnel Officer School, pretty much by default. I did not care much for any of the other officer career progression channels that were being offered at the time. Since I could not be a flying officer, there were not many really prestigious jobs remaining, certainly none with any glamour. I did not wish to be a supply officer, special services did not attract me, and I could not see myself as an Air Police Officer.

Graduation day arrived, and I found myself on the list to get a pair of bars. I had even managed to make a female "contact" while attending school. The girl was a divorcee, but she was nice, and at least I had someone who would be there to give me a kiss and pin my bars on me. Her name was Rose Wiend (mit der W pronounced as un V). She was from Germany, and had come to this country with her now <u>ex-</u>husband. I met her through a fellow classmate, who had rented an apartment for his wife in the same complex in which Rose lived. We had no more than a half a dozen dates before I had to be on my way to Personal Officer School.

With the Caddy packed with a new assortment of uniforms, all of which now sported bars except my shorts, I headed for home for a short delay in route between OCS and my next school. I was now able to puff up my chest a little more at home, and secretly wanted to put on my uniform and parade down the middle of the street. However, I don't remember even putting on my uniform while I was home. I let the pictures that had been taken for the activity book and graduation serve for that. With what seems in retrospect like little more than a "Hi!" and "Bye!" I was now on my way to Personnel Officer School.

CHAPTER ELEVEN:
PERSONNEL OFFICER SCHOOL

THE SCHOOL WAS located at Scott Air Force Base, Illinois. After the brief stop at home, I drove to Scott AFB and checked in. There were three other officers from my OCS class who had been sent to this school and we met there. One was married and accompanied by his wife. Of the remaining, one was married and unaccompanied, and two of us were unmarried, so we decided to rent an apartment together to save money. Housing for bachelor officers was crowded at the base, so they gave us certificates of non-availability, so that we could draw extra pay for off-base housing.

Belleville

Our search for an apartment led us to a large, but barren apartment over a bar in downtown Belleville, Illinois. About the only furniture were two beds, a couple of chairs and two old chests of drawers. This was pretty dismal accommodations, but we convinced each other that we would not be staying in the apartment much, except for brief periods of sleep. We made arrangements with a small restaurant next door to feed us meals in the back room and run a tab for the food. We would fall out of bed in the morning, race down the back stairs to the restaurant, eat, and go to our cars still chewing our food. We would just make it to the class at the base in time. In the evenings we would waste away many hours at the bar before grabbing a quick bite at the restaurant and going upstairs to bed … or to St. Louis.

My officer's pay had not begun arriving regularly yet, so I found myself short on funds. I walked into one of the banks in Belleville and borrowed $1,000 on the basis of my signature alone. This did much to bring home the power that those gold bars on my shoulders carried. As an enlisted man, I could not have done that.

St. Louis

One plus of the Belleville location was that it was just across the Mississippi River from St. Louis and Busch Stadium. We went to many baseball games there that summer of 1956. A minus of the location was that it was also near to the wide open town of East St. Louis, Illinois, with its strip joints and gambling parlors. We bought champagne for a lot of floozies in the hopes that they would end the evening with us. That was never to be the case. We were always dragging our tails home (alone) by dawn's early light, often too late to change our clothes for classes, and certainly too late for anything to eat to take the taste of the night's dissipation out of our mouths.

We Actually Attended School

When graduation time came it was to the utter amazement of everyone, that only three honor graduates were recognized by the Personnel Officer School. Two of them were out on the town every night, Tim McGinnis and I, and the other classmate was married and accompanied by his wife. Everyone else quietly thought a mistake had been made with Tim and me, but we assured them that beer was an excellent stimulant, and sleep only made your brain slower.

Nearly everyone graduating, and going to a first assignment, wanted to go overseas to Germany. I really didn't care that much where I went, but I had signed up for Germany. Of our class only two of us were assigned to Japan. The others received various stateside assignments, except one, who actually got his choice of Germany. I didn't know what to expect but I was willing to try anything once. JAPAN here I come.

It seemed that the three months at school passed so quickly that I hardly had time to unpack my bags before I was packing them again. This time I had to pack with an eye towards not seeing "civilization" again for two years. There was to be no returning for leaves or vacations on this unaccompanied tour.

I stopped at home again on my way through before shipping out. I left my Cadillac with the dealer from whom I purchased it with orders to sell it, and put the money in escrow for another car when I returned from Japan. Mother and Dad took me to the train, and I began the first part of my journey with a memorable trip to San Francisco on the Santa Fe Chief. By memorable, I mean not for the events, but for the beautiful scenery across the country. It was the first time that I could sit back and really enjoy the view without being in a rush, or having to look after a prisoner, or something.

CHAPTER TWELVE:
SHIPPING OUT

THE TRIP TO Japan had begun with the train trip to San Francisco, and then the long bus trip to Travis Air Force, the embarkation center. After that there were days and days of sitting around awaiting a "port call" at the out-processing center. In that time, I made friends with others who were Japan-bound. We had sufficient time to drive to San Francisco several times to see the sights and generally goof off for nearly a week. Since I had left my car behind, I had to rely upon others for a ride.

San Francisco

There was a long delay in getting orders cut and flights manifested. We were to be waiting shipment for three to four days. One fellow officer still had a car with him. He was to give it to a "hiking" service the day he shipped out. They would, for a price, ship his vehicle for him. Needless to say, he was very popular. We looked to him to get us into San Francisco each evening while we waited to ship out. San Francisco was a fun town, and all that I had heard it to be. We did it all, from the "Top O' Mark" to Fisherman's Wharf, to North Beach. It was really a wide open town in those days, and I suddenly decided that I liked it better than Chicago.

Hawaii and Wake Island

I finally got a flight assigned, and a set of orders. I was ready to go. The Orient beckoned. I had hidden memories of "Terry and the Pirates" of my comic book days floating around in the back of my mind.

The plane flight to Japan seemed never-ending. This was the age of prop planes which required stops in Hawaii and Wake Island as we made our way across the Pacific. We had to turn back to Hickham AFB when we were several hours out of Hawaii. We stayed there in Hawaii for two days while they changed an engine.

I wanted to go downtown Honolulu to see the cribs that were mentioned in the book, "Sadie Thompson." I was disappointed to learn that they had long since been closed. I did get to see a lot of the island of Oahu though, and I stuck my toe into the Pacific Ocean for the first time.

When we reached Wake Island we were delayed there for another two days while they repaired another engine. We slept in stifling hot metal huts and they had nothing but warm beer to drink. The only sights to see were piles of abandoned supplies left by the American troops during WWII and old Japanese bunkers along the shore line guarding old ship derelicts. Some of the puzzling piles of supplies were literally mountains of soles and heels for military shoes and similar mountains of porcelain bathroom fixtures. These piles of odd supplies were bigger than a two story house.

Japan

At last, Japan. Among the things which first struck me as we alit, were the strange smells. Not necessarily all bad, but certainly different. The next thing that struck me odd was the fact that it seemed that nearly everyone we passed was relieving himself or herself along the side of the road as we passed by in the bus.

We arrived at the in-processing center and found that, though everyone had been assigned to the 5th Air Force, we now had to be reassigned to individual bases according to their needs. This meant another day or two wait until we got our final assignments. It was with this wait that I was first able to venture off the base and into my first exposure to Japanese culture. I later learned that this small village of Tachikawa, near the base, was not representative of all Japanese villages, but I believed it to be at the time.

Under the guidance of an "Old China Hand," who delighted in taking new personnel to see the sights, I was able to sample some of the food and drink that was available. There were many other tidbits more attractive than the food and drink, but I felt that, one, I was an officer and a gentleman now, and two, I was not sure of the correct protocol, and three, I didn't know the rate of exchange. With all of those beautiful girls to be had for a "song," it was sort of like being a kid in a candy store and all I could do was press my nose to the glass. This was really something to write home about, but needless to say, it was something you didn't write home about. I am glad my orders came the next day or my resolve may have weakened.

In retrospect, travel was a little primitive in those days. The Air Force, with all of its planes, decided to send those of us bound for the South of Japan, by train. We ended up in the Japanese version of a Pullman car, clattering and banging our way to the Island of Kyushu. Passenger trains in Japan are models of efficiency and promptness. They do not sidetrack for freight, and they keep to a precise schedule.

I was able to see much of the countryside of Japan as we steamed along. I say steamed, because the locomotives were all coal burning steam engines. One marvel of the trip was the incredibly long rail tunnel under the sea, connecting the island of Honshu with the island of Kyushu. The conductors, attendants and other train personnel all came around and made sure that windows were closed before we entered the tunnel. The fumes and smoke from the locomotive soon seeped into the train, even with the windows closed. I could imagine what it would have been like with an open window.

CHAPTER THIRTEEN:
TSUIKI AFB

T**HE TRAIN FROM** Tokyo arrived in Fukuoka, the largest city on the island of Kyushu. From here, I was bused to Itazuke Air Force Base, located several miles south of the city. Itazuke was the home of the 43rd Air Division, which was the umbrella unit for the area. They put me up in the BOQ until someone could find out where I belonged, and could tell me what to do next. I did not know then that Tsuiki AFB, to which I was assigned, was quite remote.

When someone came to get me, I was surprised to learn that I was going to fly there by L-20. This was the first of many flights that I would be making in this small, short-runway, five-passenger aircraft. The current Personnel Officer, Lt. Hyland, whom I was to replace, had come to escort me to my new base and assignment. He was also there to pick up the payroll for his base. After we arrived at Tsuiki, he escorted me to meet my new commander, introduce me to the base staff, and to meet his Personnel Office staff.

The Personnel Office
The office seemed to be well staffed with experienced personnel. The NCO in charge had many years' experience. With his capable personnel, he could probably have taken care of the office without intervention of a Personnel Officer.

One of the staff in the Personnel Office was Lt. Hyland's secretary, Fuyo Oyake. I remember her as a very slim girl with long dark hair and a cute dimple when she smiled. Her features seemed sharper than most of the round faced Japanese girls that I had seen up until then but, beyond an acknowledgment of her presence, there was nothing made of our meeting. She seemed to regard me with no more than the casual interest of an employee looking over her next boss. Who would have known that the "boss" roles might be reversed in the years to come.

A Multitude of Jobs

One nice thing about a small base was that, because of a small staff, many officers had to double up on a number of duties and functions. I was exposed to many different jobs. Among those were: Personnel Officer, Adjutant, Air Police Officer, Censorship Officer, Cryptographic Officer, Mess Officer, Theater Officer, Voting Officer, Special Services Officer, Motor Pool Officer, Aircraft Maintenance Officer, Food Service Officer, and Base Commander. At one time I had 21 different positions assigned by orders.

All of these jobs took a certain amount of time, and it was seldom that I could take a breather during duty hours. It was hard to remember sometimes which hat I was wearing. The one that was probably the most tedious was serving as Adjutant to the CO. He was very meticulous about his correspondence and I had to compose each one of his letters. It took me a while before I was able to produce a letter without several revisions. It was not a matter of grammar, spelling, or punctuation, it was simply using the particular style that he preferred.

Tent City

All personnel on the base, officers and enlisted men alike, slept in tents. At least that is what we called those quarters. They were flimsy, wooden framed buildings with canvas roofs. The canvas was pulled tight over the frame by ropes staked to the ground. The correct military name for these quarters were "tropical barracks." The weather in southern Japan was mild, but each tent had an oil-fired space heater to take the chill off the area in cold weather. The hot chimney going up through the canvas roof, though insulated with a tin collar, was often the source of a fire on the base. Several tents had burned down.

The Base was shared by a unit of the Japanese Air Self Defense Force (JASDF), pronounced "jazzdaff." Their mission here was to learn aircraft maintenance from the U.S. Air Force, and do some basic flight training. The real title for all this activity was Rear Echelon Maintenance Combined Operation (REMCO). The Japanese troops lived in tin Quonset huts, which were hotter in summer and colder in winter than our tropical barracks.

Most of the streets on the base were paved and most of the runways were paved. The unpaved runways were surfaced with PSP, or "pierced steel planking" which was used for emergency runways during the "big war." The concrete gutters at the edges of the streets were not the usual gutter. They were two feet deep and about one foot wide. They were certainly a hazard to any airmen who wandered home late at night with a few too many drinks under his belt. The clinic did a big business in treating leg and other related injuries resulting from stepping into these gutters. One interesting thing was that during the land crab season the gutters would be nearly half full of land crabs which had wandered in while making their pilgrimage to the sea. The next rain would flush them out, but if the rains didn't come for a while the smell would get pretty ripe.

Typhoons

Another local hazard was the weather. When a typhoon warning went up, all personnel would go to one of the few solid masonry buildings on the base. They were the base operations building, the Officers Club, the enlisted men's mess hall and a building housing the base exchange. Wooden framed, single story, buildings included the Base Headquarters, the Enlisted Club, Base Supply and few other support structures. The hangers were metal, as were a few auxiliary buildings. The officers would usually go to base operations where we could keep a minute by minute update on the storm. We could watch it on radar and listen to the reports by radio.

If the hot, humid, close feeling in the air, and the overcast skies were not enough, they kept a chalkboard at headquarters to tell you when a typhoon was coming. It was updated every few hours with the latest position reports of the typhoon bearing down on Japan. In addition to the reports, my own tent-mate, 1st Lt. James, the Base Meteorologist, kept me up to date.

Although typhoons in Japan were not an infrequent occurrence, the one I experienced was aimed directly toward us. By the end of the duty day, a light rain had started and wind gusts were picking up, but not any real problems.

By the time I had eaten dinner at the Officer's club, it began to look really nasty and most of the personnel were moving to the few permanent buildings. The word went out that no one should remain in their tent until the typhoon had passed. I went to my tent and picked up a few items that I might need if I stayed elsewhere.

The rain was falling harder now, and my poncho felt like it was being pulled from me. It was certainly no weather for an umbrella. If the wind didn't tear it out of your hands the rain would have soaked you, since it was now coming at you horizontally. I made my way to base operations to wait out the storm. Most of the flying personnel were there, as well as key staff. We tried to make ourselves comfortable as the storm intensity became much stronger.

The winds were really raging, and we heard reports from some airmen, who were brave enough to be out in the wind, that we had already lost several tents. Suddenly there was an easing off of the wind and an eerie quiet descended. The weather officer quickly passed the word for everyone to stand fast, because this was simply the eye of the typhoon passing by. This warning was certainly needed for neophytes, such as myself, who thought it was over.

The silence was quickly broken by the sound of the wind picking up. This time it came at us even harder than before. Certainly, I had been raised on the plains of Kansas in tornado alley, but had never experienced a tornado, except for a few stormy threats. A typhoon is a much larger storm in area, but less powerful than the concentrated force of a tornado.

The back side of the storm was more damaging to the tents and other buildings than the first part of the storm, but it passed by much more quickly. By morning the skies had cleared and everyone crept out of their refuges to go about their daily duties. Those with much damage to their living quarters were excused to salvage what they could and prepare to move elsewhere until the damage was repaired.

My own tent was spared except that a huge tree, more than two feet in diameter, had been blown down across the entry way. Eight more inches to the left and it would have crushed the front part of the tent. I told my roommate, the weather officer, that he must have had made an inside deal with the typhoon since he could probably speak its language.

The Foreign National employees returned to work as if nothing had happened. A typhoon was old hat to them and their own buildings seemed to sustain very little if any damage. I guess they simply gave with the wind. The base was the scene of tattered strips of canvas and siding debris for several weeks following our little breeze.

I Pilot a Jet to Tokyo

The Operations Officer was Major Douglas. He was an old flyer and had flown across the English Channel during WWII. I best remember him for his ability to sing, in good voice, all of the old ribald flying songs from WWII and the Korean War. He used to keep us officers entertained for hours around the bar at the officers club. He was married to an Army nurse stationed at Camp Zama Hospital, in the Tokyo area. Nearly every Friday evening he would "borrow" a Japanese T-33 and fly to Tokyo to spend the weekend with his wife.

On one occasion I was able to hitch a ride with him. Not only was the trip simply for the thrill of my first jet ride, but to reclaim some of my belongings from a fellow officer who had refused to send me my stuff. This situation came about by reason of our having commingled a shipment of our belongings from Travis AFB, the port of embarkation, to Tokyo.

The trip was certainly a thrill. I was able to take the controls of the jet after we were in the air. The only downer was that they did not have a pilot helmet that was the right size for my big head, so I had a rotten headache for the last few minutes of each direction of the trip. Major Douglas, of course, made the approach and landed us. I was most excited about seeing Fujiyama (Mt. Fuji) at that altitude, and being able to take pictures of it from the cockpit.

I Become a Projectionist

Among the many things for which the personnel officer was responsible, was that of supervising the Base Theater. In this role I had the fun of learning how to operate the big carbon arc movie projectors and how to change the Panatar Lenses. After learning the job I would gladly fill in for the enlisted men projectionists much of the time. After all it meant a free movie. I was able to develop my skills so that I would only miss seeing a few seconds of the movie for each reel. I can recall burning a hole in only one film, and having to bring up the lights to fix something only a half dozen times at most. This was the most enjoyable additional duty I had during my entire service career.

Fuyo Oyake

My dutiful secretary would always get me a cup of coffee in the morning. Just as it was about cool enough to drink, and when I wasn't looking, she would put it back on the stove to get hot, or refill it with hot coffee from the pot. It was many years before I decided to tell her that I hated very hot coffee. I suffered in silence because I did not wish, I suppose, to disparage her efforts at serving me.

My secretary and I had few conversations then that were not related to business, but I recall once describing a movie that I had seen on the base. She had seen the movie as well, and we both related to the same feelings we had about it. The next mistake that I may have made was in being solicitous of her grief when her then boyfriend rotated back to the States. Before I knew it, I was inviting Fuyo to an occasional movie.

The Civilian Personnel Officer on the base reported to me, and I approved all payrolls and promotions. One day he notified me that his office was having a party and that I was invited as the guest of honor. When I arrived I found that I was the only American at the party. I also found that Fuyo was in attendance. She was not on his staff, so the obvious conclusion was that the occasional movie had been interpreted as something more serious, and that she was at the party as my date. I had not known about her invitation until I arrived. As with all Japanese parties there was much song and sake. When it was time to go home it was only right that I see Fuyo home.

It certainly seemed to me that someone should see her home. She had been well over-served and was very flushed and unsteady on her feet. I did not know where she lived until this evening. She directed me to her house, and then insisted that we walk off the alcohol. We made several circles of the block and nearby rice paddy before she went in. Though this night was not a "date" date, we began seeing each quite often after this.

I found that she loved to play ping pong, so I invited her and the Commander's secretary to play at the Officers Club during lunch hours. This became a daily ritual. I didn't like to play with her only because she was too good, and I didn't want to look stupid being beaten by a girl. We would camouflage this weakness by playing doubles.

Subsequently we became an item. I invited her to a big party at the Officers Club. We had hors d'oeuvres, dancing, and a stage show. Later in the evening Fuyo was hungry. She heard me ordering a "VO Sandwich" at the bar, so she ordered one also. When she was served a double VO whisky and ginger ale, she was too shy to send it back and drank it all. The results were not too pretty. Her usual drink tolerance was a teaspoon of liquor in a glass of mix. She did not get sick, at least right then, but she certainly got pretty giddy, to say the least.

By this time I had learned about Fuyo's family. The Oyake family tree was Bushi (Samurai). They were originally warriors of the Takamatsu Daimyo, but with the end of feudalism, the class system was supposed to have ended. However, the Samurai remained as judges, teachers, government officials, and captains of industry. Marriages, entry into good colleges, and employment are still determined by what name you possess.

Fuyo's great uncle was a Japanese Supreme Court justice. He was an official in Korea during the Japanese occupation of Korea. He had invited Fuyo's father to come to Korea to work for the Japanese controlled newspapers. It was in Korea that Fuyo was born. While she was growing up in this wealthy family they were afforded many perks: private schools, maids, gated housing compounds, and the like.

With the end of the war the Russians pushed south into Korea and with the freeing of the Koreans from Japanese control, the family had to flee south past the 38th Parallel. They traveled on foot through the mountains carrying their now meager belongings on their backs.

Finally passing the border, they were rescued by Americans and put on a boat back to Japan. With no clout or money remaining, the family took up residence in Nakatsu, Japan, where Fuyo finished grade school, high school, and attended night school at Kokura University. For financial reasons she had to quit school. She then went to work for U.S. Forces Japan as a supply clerk, and later as a secretary in the Personnel Office, where we met her.

The Base Closes

The first hint of a reduction of our mission at Tsuiki was that 5th Air Force stopped sending in replacements for our key positions as people rotated back to the states. The biggest gaps were left in the officer staff as I gradually picked up the jobs of the departing officers. The big job was Commanding Officer. As the last officer left who outranked me, I became the Base Commander. It soon became clear that we were not going to get replacements, and soon the official word came down that I was to take all necessary steps to close the base and return it to the Japanese.

The big job was to dispose of all supplies and facilities. Much material was given to the Japanese, but most of it was destroyed with a torch or bulldozed into the ocean. Many tough decisions were made at the top echelons regarding the value of the material versus the cost of transporting it by air or overland to another base. The shipping of people out to new assignments and the crating of records and supplies became a flurry of activity. As the numbers of personnel became fewer and fewer, those remaining had to work harder and harder to finish the mission. At last the fateful day arrived, and generals and dignitaries from both nations came to the official signing-over ceremony. The last act was bringing down the American flag and hauling up the "meatball" (the Japanese flag). My job was done.

The Overland Trip

Every other officer and enlisted man had left the base. I was to meet a truck the next morning which was to take the last load of material that had been assembled in the supply building. I gathered my gear and moved there to spend the night. I slept the night on the load of supplies that were to be transported.

I had retained a staff car, which I was then to drive to Itazuke Air Force Base after the truck departed. I was to be the last man off my "ship." I had some trepidation about the drive. It was a long trip over very bad roads and I was totally unfamiliar with the route. I had always flown to the home base, never driven.

The truck arrived early. They had driven all night. I loaded my bags in my car and prepared to leave. My first stop was to pick up Fuyo. Nearly all of the civilian employees who had been willing to relocate to Itazuke had been given a job. I had written letters of recommendation for Fuyo and a few others to assist them in being placed. Since Fuyo was moving, she asked if she could ride along with me. The long trip took the remainder of the day over those bad roads. It was well after dark when we arrived in the vicinity of Itazuke AFB.

I was driving along slowly trying to find where the turn-off was to the base. Suddenly a red light appeared in my rear view mirror. It was the Air Police. They pulled me over and asked for my trip ticket. I laughed and said, "Hell, I don't even have a motor pool." They didn't quite understand that, and I had to explain that I had driven nearly all day ... "blah, blah, blah." They were only half listening as they eyed Fuyo. They were so sure that something fishy was going on. Here I was, out on a dark road with a female Japanese National, and no trip ticket.

It seems that I had missed the turn-off and was two miles beyond it. When they finally began to believe me just a little, I asked them to please escort me to the base and to the female employees' quarters, and to give me directions to the motor pool where I was supposed to turn in my vehicle. They led me on to the base and stayed around while I dropped off Fuyo and her gear. I had to be very formal and abrupt with getting her into the new quarters, since I was under the scrutiny of the police. They followed me to the motor pool where I dumped the staff car, and they were nice enough to give me a ride to the Visiting Officer's Quarters.

Mission Accomplished

The following morning I reported to the Wing Commander. I saluted and told him, "Sir, mission accomplished, base closed." He was very non-committal about the completed project, which I felt was surely worth a medal. However, he spent a brief time with me uttering a few pleasantries. He then told me where I should report to my next assignment. He directed me to go see a Colonel Ventriss, Commander of Brady Air Force Base, and that he would have a job for me. I saluted and departed, wondering what I would be doing next. I went to the VOQ, collected my gear, and called for a staff car to take me to Brady. The base was some distance away, but I thought as one last perk as an ex-base commander, I should be driven some place in style.

The trip to Brady was north to Fukuoka, through a busy city, then several miles east over a very congested highway. The traffic consisted primarily of three-wheeled motorized trucks, usually with the load stacked twice higher than one would think safety would allow. The other component of the traffic was monstrous standard four and six wheel trucks, also piled with loads that you would think would cause the axles to snap. Filling every remaining available space on the roadway were the bicycles, tricycles and other non-motorized vehicles, which included oxcarts, and men and women walking, pulling two wheeled carts. These were nearly all piled high with goods (or people), but all scrambling to get to where they were going with a seeming disregard for life or limb.

When I arrived at Brady, I reported in to Colonel Ventriss. He was not prepared to say immediately what I was to do. He said that he needed both a Personnel Officer and a Provost Marshall. I told him that whatever he wanted me to do, I would do, while suggesting lightly that I was a trained Personnel Officer. He took my little hints as all senior officers are disposed to do, then assigned me to the position of Provost Marshall. Thankfully, I was not completely in the dark about what the duties entailed. I had performed the job as one of my additional duties at Tsuiki AFB.

CHAPTER FOURTEEN:
BRADY AFB

BRADY WAS LOCATED on a long narrow peninsula sticking out from the north end of the Island of Kyushu. There was a small fishing village at each end, and except for a narrow public road hugging the north shore, the base took the entire width of the land, from sea to sea.

Provost Marshall

I was assigned to the position at a time when the base was expending a considerable sum of money on new facilities. I was able to oversee the building of new offices for myself and staff and obtain authorization for more personnel. The last officer to hold the position was limited in resources to do any sort of a job in the security or police business.

In terms of security there was only one area that required tight security, which was the Army Security Agency's facility. This unit was a tenant on the base, and was a very hush, hush intelligence gathering operation. They had an array of all kinds of antennas and radio equipment taking up acres of open field and one top secret blockhouse. We monitored external security for that unit.

Control of base access was my responsibility, but it was the Japanese National employees who actually manned the gates. A lot of my unit's workload involved investigations of airmen engaged in black market activities, theft and other petty crimes.

One activity I did in addition to duty was to organize a base pistol team. We then went to various bases on the island for shoot-off contests to determine the championship. I still have one of my trophies turning green somewhere among my keepsakes.

Scrip Exchange Day

One of the duties of the Provost Marshall's office was to provide security for scrip exchange. Scrip was our paper money that served for U.S. Currency overseas. Scrip money is exchanged periodically to prevent black market activities, to prevent any long range counterfeit operations, and to prevent the local economy from becoming based on the current scrip issue.

All of the commanders, security personnel, and finance personnel are alerted ahead of time, but the official announcement that is made to all personnel comes with an early morning broadcast over Armed Forces Radio. At that exact same time the base is sealed and no one gets on or off without a strip search. Everyone must go to a central location with all their scrip, sign a roster, and turn in the old issue. At the end of the line a representative of finance is there to give them new money (scrip). The police have a busy day patrolling the fences.

At the end of the day any of the Japanese business people who had accepted the old scrip issue are left holding worthless paper. All knew that it was not legal to take scrip for purchases, but most of the merchants did it as a favor. There were many transactions done in scrip. The most pathetic sight was the dozens of "bar girls" willing to throw their purses over the fence to anyone who would take them. Their purses often contained literally thousands of dollars' worth of scrip.

To some it may have meant a year's work on her back, because she had not gotten around to trading in the scrip for hard currency or yen. Part of my job was to keep everyone away from the fences.

I Send for a Car

Since everyone else seemed to be doing it, I ordered a Cadillac to sell to the Japanese. The price that they were bringing on the open market was criminal. The car had to be at least two model years old and be in the seller's possession a year. The Japanese wanted the biggest car that they could get and they had to have four doors. They preferred them to be black. I ended up with a robin's egg blue one.

I made arrangements with the dealer with whom I had left my old Cadillac to find me another one. I prevailed upon my parents to make the purchase for me armed with my power of attorney. As luck would have it, my sister Ethel was getting married, and was going on her honeymoon about this time. I suggested they could have the use of my car for their honeymoon in exchange for driving it to the port and shipping it to Japan for me. I arranged for authorization.

I See Oyake-san Often

Public transportation was cheap and convenient, so Fuyo and I would frequently meet in Fukuoka for dinner and a movie. She would ride the train in from Itazuke, and I would take the bus from Brady. Even after I got my car, I didn't drive it very much. I wanted to keep it in top shape and with the bad traffic and narrow roads, I was never sure that I would not get into an accident.

In addition, there was hardly any place to park once I got off the base. Japan was not as reliant upon the automobile, so there were no accommodations for them in the way of service stations, parking spaces, etc. Fukuoka was the biggest city in Kyushu, and was loaded with places to shop, and to eat, and to be entertained. We saw a lot of first run movies. They would come to the theaters in Fukuoka before they came to the base. For my part the Japanese subtitles obscured part of the picture at times, but it was nice to stay current with all of the films.

It was about this time that I got to meet Fuyo's father and her older brother. I guess it was time for that old, "Young man, are your intentions honorable?" speech. However, the language barrier prevented any direct questions, so I sat around and smiled a lot. I think I got a free pass because the older men could relate to my being in the military with Samurai. I certainly didn't bring up that my immediate family were itinerant farmers. I got away from the meeting with a whole skin, and the relationship between Fuyo and I continued unclouded by parental wrath.

Hong Kong

The opportunity arose for an R & R (Rest & Recreation) trip to Hong Kong for those who had leave time and could break away. I quickly volunteered. The trip was mostly a non-stop shopping venture for those who could afford it. I was not very well off in that area. I was sending money home and paying for the car I had sent over.

The trip down was in a monstrous C-130 which was, at the time, the biggest cargo plane in the regular inventory of the Air Force. It was turbo prop plane, the noisiest means of transportation known to man. I pounded wax-impregnated cotton into my ears and could not keep the sound out. It seemed to come through my bones. When we finally landed, I could not hear properly for hours. During the landing we hit the runway very hard. The pilot had not landed at Kai Tak, Kowloon (Hong Kong) before. I learned that we had actually cracked the runway, and that further landings of this particular type of aircraft were forbidden.

The Hong Kong trip was quite an adventure. I bought a couple of suits, and since most all of us on the trip had suits and jackets tailored at the same place, the tailor shop served as tour guide and entertained us for most of the time we were there. My few additional purchases consisted of an ivory chess set and a pair of shoes made to my measurements while I was there. I was amazed with the different foods, and was able to take part in three major banquets: one in a white linen restaurant, one a traditional Chinese dinner in a big hotel overlooking Hong Kong harbor and one on the "Princess" floating restaurant in Aberdeen.

One interesting place we visited was called "The Hanging Gardens." The interior was very flowery and garden-like, and the decor was beautiful. The interesting part was that the place had two menus, one for drinks, and one for "flowers" (no food). Each "flower" had a name, a country of origin, and a short physical description. There were blacks, whites, Latins, Eurasians, Chinese, and the whole range of feminine pulchritude from which to select. The idea was that you ordered a drink, and you ordered a "flower." She would sit with you, at the rate indicated on the menu, and converse in the language of your choice until you were ready to leave. This was not a high class brothel. I suppose that arrangements were possible, but that was not condoned by the management. No girl could be seen leaving with a customer. We drank, but had no conversation with any of them. We were too cheap on the one hand, and preferred filling our eyes rather than our ears on the other.

It took two trucks to haul everything our little group purchased back to the cargo plane when we left. Some people bought a lot of stuff. One guy drove an English sports car on board. They were cheap and tax free.

The Busy B Club

An interesting circumstance which I mention, only because it was reminiscent of a situation from my "B Hive" school days, occurred at Brady. There were four of us officers holding key position on the base whose names began with the letter "B": Beers of the Motor Pool, Bramman of Special Services, Bradley of Food Services and Club Officer, and Bishop the Provost Marshall. There were only two other officers, the commander and the Supply Officer; the Supply Officer didn't count, because he was only a warrant officer.

We called ourselves the "Busy Bees" and were often to be found at our regular meeting place, "The Boom Boom Room." The BOOM of that name for the bar was from "Brady Officer's Open Mess," which was the official name of the officers club.

We went bar hopping together, sightseeing together, and had parties together for the nurses and ladies from Special Services who were stationed there. We really had nothing in common except for the happenstance of being assigned together at the same base (and the B in our last name).

The Slicky Boy

At one period during my tour at Brady, things were starting to disappear from the officer's quarters rooms. Several officers were missing things at night while they slept. I told everyone to take better precautions with their doors and to make the proper reports of their losses. I did not get overly concerned until my leather jacket and wallet were taken. There was nothing in the wallet but a few hundred yen, but I was highly miffed.

It was not until several weeks later that a Captain from the Army security unit caught the guy red handed. He physically held him until I took over and got my police people to take him for questioning. Since he was a Japanese National, we notified the local police who then took over with the "interrogation." They moved him to their small police station in the village where they were able to bounce him around a bit. He admitted that evening's intrusion, but would not admit to having been on the base before.

I went with the local police as they were to transport him to a larger Prefecturate jail. It was a cool night, and on the way the thief asked to pick up his jacket where he had left it in the bushes off base, along with some of his belongings. I was in the staff car at the time. The thief came out of the weeds carrying his stuff and wearing *my* leather jacket. When I told the police chief this information, the slicky boy (local slang for a clever burglar or crook) got his head beat in with a truncheon, not because it was my jacket, but because he had been lying to the police. They did not take kindly to that.

I Sell My Car

When I had owned the car for the requisite one year, I put out the word that it was available for sale. I certainly wanted to have it sold before I returned to the states. I had waited so long to have a car sent over, that time was becoming a factor in getting rid of it. Through an interpreter at my office I was able to make contact with a president of a coal mining company, or I should say, I was put in contact with his intermediaries. When the day of the appointment came, I took the interpreter along and went to the designated location. A staff of people was there to meet us. Two chauffeurs and a minor vice president were to go along for the demonstration ride along with the president of the company.

When the VIP finally came out, everyone became very busy and officious. The VIP was ushered into the back seat, and I was directed to take off very quickly and go around the block. When I returned, I showed all of them the automatic trunk closer. It was a fairly new feature to automobiles. When the trunk lid barely touched the closing latch, a screw mechanism engaged and pulled the trunk closed with a very mechanical buzzing and a satisfying click. Everyone seemed to go gaga over this feature. Even the VIP flickered a bit of interest. The VIP went into his office and I never saw him again. I didn't know whether I had made a sale or not.

My interpreter and I cooled our heels for a while, then after some time, two people came out of an inner office carrying a huge yellow envelop. It was full of money. I didn't know whether I was to spend the rest of the afternoon counting it or whether I was to take the money and run. I asked the interpreter what I should do. He suggested that we simply count a couple of packets as a spot check of the amount and then graciously bow and depart. We quickly made a cursory count, smiled, bowed and left. There were no papers signed.

I now was sweating out how to get $16,000 in very negotiable currency home without being hit over the head for it. I needn't have worried, but I was nervous. I really didn't draw a relaxed breath until I had it all locked into my safe at the office. I had received three times what the car cost me.

My next job was to turn all that Japanese yen into scrip, which I could turn into greenbacks, which I could then ship home. I put the word out that anyone needing yen to go shopping (or to give to their girlfriend), I was available for exchanging money.

Pay Officer

About this time, the Commander decided that he would maintain a large quantity of scrip and yen on the base so that we would not have to make a special trip to Itazuke every two weeks to pick up the payroll. We would simply make up the payroll from cash on hand. That cash was to be kept in a huge Japanese safe that they had located somewhere. They made hole in the side of the headquarters building, and moved the safe into a small office on the ground floor. Getting the safe into place took more than a week.

As the next step, the Colonel assigned me as the part-time "banker" for the base. I was to make an occasional trip for cash then pay the troops on paydays. I also kept open an hour each day for those who wished to exchange scrip for yen. The big customers were the service clubs, but some individuals purchased yen from my "bank."

With this turn of events, I had solved my problem of how to get rid of my own personal foreign currency from the sale of my car. I asked the Commander if I could commingle my money with the other money in the safe so that I could get rid of my yen. He agreed, but I must admit that we both knew that it violated good financial practices, and may have even been illegal.

The Big Question

I think that Fuyo only half believed me when I made it official and told her that I would come back for her. Even after I had shopped for about the largest diamond that I felt that I could afford at the time, and had put it on her finger, I was not sure that she was all that convinced of my intentions. I have a picture of her taken the evening that I popped the question to her. She looks awfully pensive in that picture. She "went along with the gag" though, and put up a pretty good front. I'm still not sure that she believed that we would be married until it really happened and all of the papers had been signed.

Both of us had seen a lot of overseas romances end with the guy waving bye-bye, and never being heard from again. Of course, there were also lots of marriages. Unfortunately, a lot of those were between young kids who were not very experienced, and were caught in the wiles of scheming girls who wanted to go to the "Land of the Big BX."

What were my thoughts about marriage? Like many, I guess, there were self-doubts and fear of the unknown. Was I simply getting old enough that it was the thing to do? Had I become tired of searching or merely jaded? Was it propinquity, or was I living out the childhood fantasy for an Oriental female *a la* "Terry and the Pirates?"

Back to the States

When my assignment to go back to the states came through I was surprised to learn that I was being reassigned in my Air Police specialty, and not in Personnel, the field in which I had received training. The next surprise was that I was returning to Francis E. Warren Air Force Base after an absence of only a little more than three years.

My preparations were mostly a flurry of purchasing stuff, since I now had a little more money to do that, and then the packing up all that stuff to send home. Some of the purchases were made with the intention of using them in a new household so Fuyo had some input on those. The base carpenters built a huge shipping crate for my household goods, and it was shipped by boat and by train, until it finally ended up on the platform at the train station at Cassoday, Kansas. I don't know how Dad got that huge container on his truck, but I know how he got it off. He tied a chain around it and a tree then drove away. He had, of course, opened the container and removed the contents. I remember that huge container setting in the yard by that tree for years there on the farm. Most of the stuff sat on the screened porch for many months until I got home to open the smaller footlocker-size wooden boxes they had built for me.

With teary goodbyes to all, especially to Fuyo, I boarded a plane for the U.S.A. It had been a thirty months tour. I had voluntarily extended twice, once for a year, and once for six months. They cut short the six months tour by a little because of my orders. I guess they were hustling me along because of their perceived need of my position in Strategic Air Command Security. Bye bye, Japan, hello, Frances E. Warren

CHAPTER FIFTEEN:
F. E. WARREN REVISTED

FRANCIS E. WARREN was no longer an Air Training Command Base, but was now a part of the Strategic Air Command. Many of the temporary barracks that had housed the training squadrons were now torn down and permanent brick and steel structures supporting the Atlas missile program stood in their place.

Without the thousands of young Airmen in various training courses flooding into Cheyenne, the city seemed a little cleaner, somehow, and for some strange reason a little more prosperous. The new military population for the base was a little older, mostly married with families, and with more money to spend. Base housing could no longer support the numbers of married personnel so many families were living in the surrounding community.

I Become an Air Police Officer

I was not to be a Provost Marshall; I was to be a Director of Security and Law Enforcement. The names and classifications had changed. The current officer in the position was retiring. He was an older captain who had been called back from the reserves for the Korean conflict. We hit it off well and my indoctrination went very smoothly.

Two things happened almost simultaneously. Another officer was assigned to the base with the same specialty. He was put over me since he outranked me by two grades. Now, instead of reporting to the Base Commander, I would now be reporting to him. The increased emphasis on security of the weapons systems caused SAC to rethink the law enforcement and security mission. The other event was the reassignment of another officer to head up a new security squadron. I was now on the bottom of the totem pole with only the Air Police as my responsibility.

The "Q"

I took quarters in the Bachelor Officer Quarters. I had been spoiled overseas from having everything so convenient and inexpensive. Plus the fact that I had had a house boy (or, on some occasions, a house girl) who nearly did everything for me, washing and ironing clothes, cleaning my rooms, making my bed, and nearly everything but cooking my meals.

For the "Q," most of my meals consisted of baloney and cheese sandwiches, washed down with Tang. Other officers in my organization were married, thus lunched at home rather than at the club. With no car, this meant a long walk to the club or a shorter walk to the "Q" for a sandwich.

For entertainment I didn't have a radio or a TV, so it would have been pretty boring if I had not liked to read. I also wrote a lot of letters. Fuyo kept up her end of the bargain and wrote often.

I Get Another Car

Without a car I was confined to the base and had to walk to work. I needed to put an end to that quickly. I had to have a car. I took a bus to town, and resolved not to ride a bus back. I walked to as many car dealerships as I could shop. There are a lot of used car lots in a service town. I bought a "new" car all right. It was a ten year old Chevrolet sedan. I got a terrific buy on it. I offered a rock-bottom price, and the salesman, thinking that he might stick me for long interest payments to make up for his low price, was surprised when I paid cash for it and drove it away. I now could get around the base and eat regular breakfasts in the mess hall, and take lunch and dinner in the Officer's Club. This was a pleasant change from baloney sandwiches three meals a day.

The car was in better condition than I thought. It served me faithfully through several trips home. The drive home and back certainly took longer than in my old Cadillac, and I didn't get the mileage, but the car made the trips without burning too much oil.

I Move to Security

I did not get on well with the new director, a Major and a little Napoleon. He was so nit-picky about everything that I thought that I was back in OCS. The new Security Squadron was now getting organized. New enlisted security personnel were arriving and training, housing, and other administration for to all these personnel required a large support staff. The Director took this opportunity to send me to the Security Squadron as an operations officer. I was happy to get from under his direct supervision.

The job of missile, warhead, and missile launch site security was very difficult to train into the new people. The work produced no tangible product, so the airmen had to constantly be reminded that they were providing a real and necessary service.

One incident, which reflected a lack of real understanding of the weapons system, involved a foot sentry at a missile site. The Atlas missiles were housed in coffin-like emplacements and were raised to launch position hydraulically. Stacked along the sides of the "coffins" were large tanks of compressed nitrogen gas, under tremendous pressure. This gas served to actuate some of the hydraulic systems and to purge the missile fuel tanks as was necessary. The sentry, patrolling the site one late night, heard a high pitched hissing. He walked along the nitrogen piping, rubbing his hands along the pipes in an attempt to locate what he felt sure was a leak. There was a leak. The escaping gas was under such pressure that it cut his fingers off cleanly. The gas was also so cold as it escaped that he did not know that he had lost his fingers for some minutes.

Married? ... Me!!??

Soon after getting organized on the base, I began work to finish the pile of paperwork which was required for Fuyo and I to get married. The marriage of a military person to a foreign national is a lot more complicated than for any private citizen. The time remaining on the Japan assignment had not been sufficient to complete the paperwork there, after I had finally made up my mind to pop the question.

During the course of the delay, I was routinely exposed to American women through work and at the club and, whether it was consciously or unconsciously, I made mental comparisons in order to justify or repudiate the decision I had made in Japan. I did not find any reason to rue the position I had taken. Their features were coarse, language harsh, and demeanors not demure.

Final approvals came through, and I made plans to return to Japan in August. Arranging for a space available flight back was quite a chore. I got to Hawaii on a SAC plane, but I could go no further because Military Air Transport Service would not accept a SAC leave form. I had to go to 5th Air Force Headquarters in the dead of night to get special orders cut.

Since I had missed the regular MATS flight, I had to look around for other means of transportation.

I finally located a C-54 that was going my way. It was a heavily equipped VIP plane, loaded with kitchen, bedrooms, and all the conveniences of home. There was no VIP aboard. The plane was being ferried to Korea for a general. There were about eight other passengers that were getting a "hop" and there were four crew members. About four hours out of Honolulu, we developed engine trouble, and we started to go back. However, we had been outrunning a typhoon, and now the typhoon cut us off from returning to Hawaii. The only alternate strip available to us was Johnson Island, several hundred miles south of Hawaii. We headed for there.

A second engine then began to act up and we then lost altitude. We even moved our baggage and other non-essential gear to the doors in readiness to jettison it if we got too low. We were almost at wave tops when we found the runway at Johnson. The island was very small; the runway started at the beach and ended at a beach about a mile later. It took the full length of the island. Our landing was pretty uneventful, but all of the people stationed there came out in their shorts and tennis shoes to welcome us. The base commander had a ball cap with his insignia on. This was the only way to tell him from any of the enlisted men in their shorts. I found out the next day the night uniform was the day uniform as well.

The quarters on the island were not very comfortable and there was nothing to do. We waited for a plane to ferry in an engine or two. After a couple of days, a mail and supply plane came in, and all of the passengers of the C-54 piled in for the trip back to Hawaii. The crew had to stay with the plane. In Hawaii I found another flight, after a day and a half, and I was on my way again.

I called Fuyo when I arrived in Japan and we made rapid plans for the event. We went shopping for a wedding dress, trousseau, and odds and ends. We got our picture taken, and I arranged for a church wedding, and lined up someone to stand up for us. Finally, on August 14, 1959, we were married three times. First we were married at the American Consulate, in a civil ceremony, then we went to the City Hall of Fukuoka for the Japanese civil ceremony, and then in the evening we were married in the Chapel at Brady Air Force Base.

To friends and anyone else who would listen to our tale, we would tell everyone, that since we were married three times we would have to be divorced three times and the hassle wasn't worth it. We had a party after our wedding ceremonies at the officer club, where a lot of our friends toasted our health until late. Our best man and matron of honor took us to Fukuoka where we caught a train to a hot springs for the first night of our honeymoon. The next day we went to Unzen, a famous park and hot springs, for most of our short honeymoon. While in that area we went to see Fuyo's aunt, uncle, and sister in Hita for the first time. The uncle asked us what we wanted for a wedding gift. Since Fuyo's family was Samurai class going back for many hundreds of years, she wanted a samurai lance that had been in the family for many generations. This would have been very difficult to bring out of the country, so we settled for an antique *kakejiku* (picture scroll) that had been in the family for a couple of hundred years. After our short honeymoon, I flew back to the States a married man. I had to leave Fuyo behind until she had obtained a passport and visa.

Now that I was married, and no longer a single entity, I could not only relate my own exploits, but must now include those of my wife (and later my family) as well. It is with this in mind that I move to Part IV of my narrative, "Twin Threads." I considered the title "Wife and Warfare," but that might be interpreted incorrectly. I simply liked the sound of the alliteration, which suggested a wife or family life on the one hand, and military life, or "warfare" on the other. It did not to mean that wife and warfare had a cause and effect relationship, **or did it?**

And so, to Part IV, "Twin Threads."

PART IV:
TWIN THREADS

MILITARY LIFE WAS now more than just a military life, I also had a family life. I had responsibilities, I had bills to pay, I had cradles to rock, and I had more to think about than just myself. I had not really prepared myself for married life. I guess that's what happens when one stays single too long.

CHAPTER SIXTEEN:
FUYO JOINS ME

Seattle, Washington

I GOT THE arrival schedule for the Fuyo's ship, the General Mann, and arranged to meet her in Seattle. You've heard of expectant fathers pacing the floor. I was an expectant husband, and was pacing the reception area until the ship docked and my new bride debarked.

Fuyo seemed kind of dazed by it all when I first saw her, but this was due to her having been sea sick for most of the voyage. I had arranged for a hotel, and she went right to bed and slept for what seemed like ages. When she could stir around again, I booked a flight back to Cheyenne, Wyoming, and I subjected her to the age old custom of carrying her across the threshold when we arrived at our new home.

Our First Home

Before Fuyo arrived, I had acquired base housing. It was a two bedroom bungalow built on a slab. There wasn't any furniture, but I had begun to get the quarters habitable. The Office of Housing Supply had any number of things that could be rented for the residence: dishes, tableware, utensils, beds, chairs, and so on.

Though I rented most everything else, I did purchase an electric can opener and a dinette set. This was what Fuyo owned to start housekeeping with when I carried her over the threshold. The can opener still works. Over fifty years later it's in better working order than I am.

During the ensuing weeks, we were making frequent trips to Cheyenne to purchase household goods. I wanted Fuyo to be in on the selection, thus my delay in buying anything much. At least I think she believed that story.

Bringing Fuyo Home to the Family

It was Thanksgiving before we could make a trip home to see my parents and I could show off my new wife to the family. Dad, unflappable Dad, welcomed her with open arms. So did Mother, but only in the literal sense, it seemed to me. Under the surface I felt that there was a little of this, "What is this foreign female doing with her hooks in my son." I know that Fuyo was anxious to be accepted and nervous about how the visit would go. I was also a bit on edge, but didn't want to admit it to anyone, including myself.

Almost before we were aware of what causes these things, as the old expression goes, we were pregnant, or at least Fuyo was. I am almost positive that the baby was conceived at my parents' house in Kansas, but Fuyo is still not so sure.

Fuyo started becoming ill almost at once. We took long rides to the country and various places to take her mind off her tummy. I can still remember going wading in a cold mountain stream after a moccasin, where she had lost it while we were crossing a foot bridge in Pole Mountain National Park.

As the pregnancy progressed, Fuyo began having more and more problems, and was hospitalized a long time before her term. We lost the baby, and it was very gloomy around our household for quite a while.

Shopping For a Car with Fuyo

Our old Chevy was getting a lot of miles on it and it was time to get rid of it. We decided to go shopping for a new one. I wanted a little bigger car, but Fuyo fell in love with a little Buick Special. It was bronze brown with the little fake port holes on the side of the hood. It was underpowered, but Fuyo liked it. She also liked the smooth salesman who bought us lunch. He pushed the car very hard after he saw that she liked it. Needless to say, we drove the car home. I missed the opportunity to show Fuyo how to dicker and deal for an auto, but what the heck. The car ended up lasting us for quite a while, including trips from coast to coast.

Fuyo's Accident

Not accustomed to simply sitting around the house, and not wanting to go to the Officer Wives Club all the time, Fuyo searched for things to do to stay busy. She enrolled in a cake decorating class and a sewing class.

In the meantime a neighbor, a major's wife, had taken Fuyo under her wing and was teaching her "American cooking."

One evening, while waiting for Fuyo to return from one of her classes in town, there was a terrible racket, and Fuyo stumbled in the door crying her head off. I wondered what the problem was until, through all of the crying, I heard the word "accident."

When I satisfied myself that she was not hurt, I looked at the car. I found it on the neighbor's lawn three doors away. She had held herself together until she got within sight of the house then lost control of herself and the car.

She had managed to stop the car before hitting anything. The door on the right side had been caved in. I wondered what could have happened. She was now able to explain that she was not in the car at the time of the accident. While she had been parked downtown near the school, a car had rolled down a sloping driveway and crossed the street and caved in the door. She came out of her class to find the damage and a note from the owner of the other vehicle.

I removed the car from my neighbor's lawn, and drove it home. I made a call to the driver of the car and exchanged insurance information. He assured me that there would be no problem. Fuyo told me later that she was more afraid of my wrath for having damaged our new car than anything, but it was an unavoidable accident on her part, so she should not have been so concerned. I did my best to allay her fears.

The Officer's Wives Cub

In our little love nest, I told Fuyo that she would have to face the Officer's Wives Club and should be prepared to join the various functions in which they participated. Bridge and mahjong were the two major games the ladies played.

I began with teaching her "honeymoon bridge," or bridge for one couple. When she learned the fundamentals, we played with friends, and I turned her loose. I had created a monster. In later years, she became a director of her own bridge group at a local country club, and we even went so far as to play in a regional tournament or two. In what I can call the present, she plays bridge three or four times a week.

Fuyo soon became comfortable with the wives club and the various protocols involved, some of which she found amusing. She was always telling me how the ones who poured the coffee out ranked the ones who poured the tea and how the pecking order of the club matched the rank of the ladies' husbands. It wasn't long before she was socializing more and more with the other wives and joining their afternoon sangria parties.

Study, Study, Study

Among other avenues of attempted escape from my top level supervisor I began applying for various positions, such as Attaché, Investigator with the Office of Special Investigations, and the like. During this time I began to spend a lot of valuable family time studying. I enrolled in several college correspondence courses and courses offered by the Air Force Institute of Technology. My intent was to be qualified for a temporary duty, called Final Semester TDY. This was offered to qualified officers who lacked a few credits of obtaining their under-graduate degree.

The degree had to be in a field related to your duties, so it could not be in basket weaving or golf. Since my acceptable credits were all over the place, I began to concentrate on Public Administration which gave a minor in Police Management and Administration.

When I had completed the magic number of required courses, I applied for the "college completion" program. It was some months before I received a reply, but then it was rush, rush, rush. I had not even known what institution I would attend until I received the letter of notification. It was to be the University of Southern California.

California, here we come!!!

CHAPTER SEVENTEEN:
USC

FUYO AND I drove across the country to California in August of 1961. It was a pretty miserable trip. Our little Buick Special had no air condition, and we were traveling with our cat, Miiko, and some potted plants, neither of which enjoyed the trip.

Coming into the Los Angeles area, for the first time in my life I was confronted with freeway traffic. It was a Sunday afternoon and there were eight lanes of nothing but solid cars and trucks. I gripped the wheel and travelled in the far right lane thinking that I would never make it to our destination. It was but a few weeks later that I was tearing along in the left lanes, keeping up with the best of them.

After a couple of day's search we found a lovely apartment in the Baldwin Hills area of southwest Los Angeles, only minutes from the university. I enrolled very quickly and began school. Fuyo, ever the industrious wife, got a job as a policy typist with Zenith Insurance Company. Her commute was longer than mine, but she quickly got used to bus schedules, transfers, and the like.

She did not work there long before she quit to move to the Pacific Indemnity Insurance Company. It was the same work for more money, a shorter commute, and much more glamorous. "More glamorous" were her words. The office was located on Wilshire Boulevard. She said it was all she could do to keep from spending all she made at all the fine shops there. Now we felt really good about ourselves. We were now DINKS (Double Income, No Kids).

I took a double load of course work so I could finish the program on time. I did not want to be so close to a degree and leave without obtaining one. While working, Fuyo was also studying for her citizenship test. She wanted to take it while we were in Los Angles. She passed the test, and I took time off from school to attend her swearing in ceremony. So it was, on January 25, 1963, Fuyo became a U.S. citizen.

The Christmas of '62, my parents came to LA by train to visit us. It was the furthest either of them had been away from home. We showed them all the sights to include Disney Land. We put them on the train and a few weeks later I graduated. I made the honor society for public administration, Pi Sigma Alpha, and I graduated *magna cum laude*.

After graduation we went back to Japan on Air Force "Space Available" transportation for a visit. We made good connections and had a wonderful time in Japan. Upon our return we were to report to our next duty station, which was to be Griffiss AFB, at Rome, New York. Once more I was to be a Law Enforcement and Security Officer.

CHAPTER EIGHTEEN:
GRIFFISS AFB

WHEN FUYO AND I arrived at Griffiss, we were welcomed with open arms. The Director, Major John R. Armstrong, and his wife, were very friendly and extremely helpful in getting Fuyo and I settled in. Major Armstrong was a flying officer during the Big War, and had been recalled to duty during the Korean conflict. He had decided to stay in the service and do his twenty.

I took up duties as OIC of the law enforcement activities. The majority of the personnel were civilians who served as gate guards and as security personnel for old AA sites. The few enlisted military police were primarily traffic patrolmen and security for the nuclear weapons site. There was a Strategic Air Command unit as a tenant on the base. It was a bomber unit and the aircraft were nuclear armed. We provided security for the weapons storage site. SAC provided their own security personnel for the aircraft.

The duties were routine except for about a bimonthly exercise regarding a simulated accident involving transporting a nuclear warhead. There were usually lots of folks standing by with clipboards, and mistakes could cost a senior person a career. The Major and I always escaped with a whole skin, but there were others who didn't fare so well.

The news got out that there were nuclear weapons on the base, so a protest group of "Peaceniks" attempted to enter the base. We held them up at the gates, and prevented a few rushes of those trying to scale the fence. It was a rather hectic ordeal for a while.

The let-down of tension after an incident is often solved by a few drinks on the patio, mowing the lawn, taking a drive, or what have you. It was only a few weeks after this that Fuyo felt the need for a doctor's appointment. Yes, she was pregnant.

Starting a Family

Our first pregnancy had been welcomed, but unplanned. We had let nature take its course. We were both happy about it, but with Fuyo having been ill during most of the pregnancy, it was almost as if she had been allergic to the fetus. We had lost the baby right at term. I had taken Fuyo to the hospital with labor pains, but it the baby was stillborn. The little girl never took a breath.

Here at Griffiss we had begun again in earnest to start a family. There were tube blockages and other little problems that had to be dealt with first. When we got the good news about the second pregnancy we were elated. The gestation period after that was fairly normal with a near term delivery. Lisa Naomi was born in the base hospital on March 5, 1964. We had chosen a middle name that was both Japanese and "mainstream."

The baby was fine, but when it came time to take them home, there were complications with Fuyo. I could only bring the baby home since the hospital had no provisions for keeping well babies.

We had already laid in lots of baby supplies, but since the baby had no mother for nursing, I had to make a mad dash to get bottles, nipples, sterilizers, and formula before I stopped by the hospital to bring Lisa home.

At home, I put Lisa in her crib at the foot of our bed. While she slept, I lay on the bed fully clothed, attuned to the slightest whimper, so I could respond instantaneously. For nearly two weeks I slept with my clothes on. If I were feeding or walking the baby, I had Lisa in one hand and "Dr. Spock" in the other. This was before the age of disposable diapers, so was much of my time was devoted to washing diapers.

When I brought Fuyo home at last, I was the one who had to teach her how to take care of her baby. We did not have parents near, and I had not wanted to impose on friends and neighbors for tasks fraught with responsibility. The Armstrongs, who had been treating us as if we were family, served as godparents when the time came for Lisa's christening.

Temporary Duty

One thing I was able to do while at Griffiss was to attend some pretty prestigious short courses in a temporary duty status. The first was Counter Insurgency School at The Air War College, Maxwell AFB, near Montgomery, Alabama. Maxwell is the home of the Air University. Most of the course material was classified, and even though it has been a while,

I doubt if anything has been declassified. One thing that wasn't too "hush hush" was our flight to Hurlburt AFB, Florida, near Elgin AFB, where we were able to observe short take-offs and landings of C-130s, after dark, and in blackout conditions. We also observed fluorescent pamphlet drops under nighttime conditions. The pamphlet drop simulated counter insurgency distribution of propaganda.

The second course was a short course in forensics for police officers, held in Washington, D.C. Both military and civilian police personnel attended. The course work covered the kind of stuff later popularized on the CSI television programs.

The third course was much longer and more complex. It was an eight credit hour college graduate school course in Criminology and Penology. It was given by the American University, of Washington D.C. and its professors lectured for the course. The course required the students to take housing in D.C. for the duration of the intensely accelerated course. I found an Army Provost Marshal that agreed to share an apartment with me, and we found a nice walkup on F Street, only a block from our "downtown" campus.

In addition to assimilating the knowledge, we had to produce a paper to graduate. To make things a little easier, we were allowed teams of three or four to cooperate on the material. The course was headed by a Professor Howard Gill, who has published many books on Penology. He was once a warden of a prison, and was then the go-to person for all things penological. His remarks in the back of our paper were, "Good work, the best paper yet." We were very proud of that. He was a tough old bird. His famous words were, "Prisoners cannot be rehabilitated; they can only be retrained."

Fuyo flew down to visit me in D.C. for a day or two during the course. She was later somewhat sorry for taking the trip. Lisa, still a baby in arms, was feverish and crying on the plane, both flying down and back. Plus, I had to force my roommate to bunk with someone else while she stayed over. He was not very appreciative of that.

Not long after the incident, Major Armstrong decided to retire. He had arranged for a reassignment to the West Coast so he could look for permanent housing before retirement. We hated to see him and his family leave, but this meant that I was the new Director of Security and Law Enforcement for the base. I didn't hold the position long before I learned that I was in line for a position with the Inspector General's office, which was quickly interrupted by the news that I needed one more overseas tour to qualify for the position. So this meant the next orders I saw was for reassignment to Korea.

The tour in Korea would be unaccompanied, so Fuyo and I had to face the fact that we would be separated for a while. We discussed where she wanted to live during the eleven to thirteen months I would be gone. There were three possibilities: She could go back to Japan and stay with her sister (or get an apartment there), she could live with my parents for that period, or she could stay in the area in a rented apartment. Since she had made some friends in the area and would be close to facilities on the base, she decided to stay in Rome, New York.

We embarked on an apartment hunting tour and decided on a large, fairly modern complex near the base and local shopping. She would have the car and could get around easily.

CHAPTER NINETEEN:
LAND OF THE MORNING CALM

WE SAID OUR tearful good-byes and I departed for Korea. I landed at a small base outside of Seoul, Korea and was met by the Director of Security and Law Enforcement and the top NCO of the Air Police Unit. We had a long Jeep ride south to my new base of assignment, Osan Air Base.

Osan: K-55

Osan Air Base was known as K-55 during the height of the Korean War. I could never figure out why a military installation was put so far away from everything. The logistics to supply the base was a big problem. Everything had to be trucked in on very primitive roads. Cargo that came by air was mail, nuclear war heads and other war materials.

My assignment was to be Operations Officer. This meant that I was in charge of both the Air Police and Security, at least for the time being. A junior officer had the job of Air Police Officer and reported to me. I had the responsibility for security directly. Another officer was assigned later in my tour to take over the security end of things. The job was not taxing mentally. My main concern was to ensure that the nuclear war heads were secure, since the Koreans were not very happy that we had a nuclear capability in their country. The second was to keep down the petty thefts and some things not so petty. Every Korean that worked on the base was suspect of sneaking things off the post.

The Theft Problem

On an occasional strip search we would find a Mama-san with rolls of toilet paper wrapped around her under her clothes. The idea was that after she got home she would unroll it onto salvaged empty rollers and then sell it on the streets.

One old man was assigned to clean up around the base and would take the leaves and twigs home in a big 55 gallon drum fastened to an "A-frame." This device was carried on the shoulders. The Koreans moved everything in that manner. The guards got tired of going through his trash every evening and would pass him through. One evening, however, he seemed to be puffing a little, so they looked under the leaves and twigs and found a Jeep engine. One theft ring we cracked was headed by an ROK (Republic of Korea) OSI (Office of Special Investigations) officer. With his official vehicle he was able to get lots of electronic equipment past the guards.

Flying above the 38th Parallel

We had a unit on base that had the mission of gathering photo intelligence of activities in North Korea. They flew unarmed C-47s across the border on almost daily flights. Once in a while they would take non-crew members along for a ride into enemy territory. I bummed a ride one time and was fascinated to see SAM sites on the ground tracking our flight path. We flew low enough that they could have shot us down easily if we had provoked them in any way.

After each flight they would develop the pictures and interpret them to determine if there had been any troop movements, by counting the number of skid marks on their runways, looking for tracks of heavy equipment, etc. Since each flight was over enemy territory, each crew member gained points for air medals with each mission. They were authorized many medals before they rotated to their next assignment.

Different Way of Life

It was obvious that the Koreans did not have quite the way of doing things that we did. I was able to observe this firsthand on several occasions. At ROK police guard mount, when the captain of the guard would inspect his troops, if something didn't suit him he would knock the soldier down to the ground. The ROK would watch us have our guard mount and would probably snicker at how soft we were with infractions.

The things that were stolen on the base passed through several hands before being sold openly on the street in little stands. It was almost as if they were thumbing their noses at us. The articles were mostly petty, such as soap, toilet paper, pencils, note paper, small radios, watches, rings, and the like. Some military personnel were fortunate enough to buy back items that had been stolen from them. Americans soon learned not to wear loose rings or expansion bracelet watches. They would be stripped off one's wrist or fingers, and the young pickpocket would be lost in the crowd. Young boys would snatch lighted cigarettes out of stroller's hands and those would be put out and sold 'as is' or rerolled in new paper and sold.

Special Services

The Special Services Office on the base provided many projects tours and hobby opportunities. The first of these I took advantage of was a tour to Pan Mun Jam, and the demilitarized zone at the 38th parallel. It was a long drive on the bus, but I did get to see the wide expanse of the "zone," the watch towers, and the conference table.

It was interesting, but not as interesting as the apocryphal tale of the U.S. Army foot patrol walking his side of the zone, dropping a shiny Zippo lighter from his pocket as if by accident. Then later at night there would be several U.S. rifles trained upon the spot when a Korean foot patrol would endeavor to pick it up.

One of the services in which I participated, was the Lapidary Workshop. They taught us how to grind and facet gemstones, both precious, and semiprecious. I made bracelets and rings of several different gemstones for Fuyo, friends, and family. After cutting and polishing, I would have the finished product set in Korean gold (at a price, of course). The Korean gold was real gold but it had an orange color, rather than the bright yellow of American gold.

Another service offered was a dubbing center. You could bring in blank reel-to-reel tapes and they would dub any selection of music, plays, or humor. Since I had purchased an expensive stereo tape player during my tour in Japan, I really loaded up on more tape than I could play in ages. I know they were violating all kinds of copyright laws, but it was all for the poor serviceman overseas. The upshot of this was that I got little use of the tapes. Cassettes and then CDs soon became the go-to source for at-home music and the like.

Another recreational service provided was transportation to approved R&R sites in Japan and Walker Hill in Korea. My R&R to Japan was to purchase lots of Japanese items that Fuyo could not purchase in the states. She had given me a list and then made an arrangement with a friend of hers in Japan to accompany me. We "shopped 'til we dropped." The load of stuff I brought back looked like enough to open a store myself.

One other trip I made to Japan was not through Special Services, but for reason of going to Tokyo for a Shrine Initiation. I had been invited to join the Ancient Arabic Order of the Mystic Shrine, a fun-making and charitable organization offshoot of the Masonic order.

Time to Rotate

The year seemed to pass quickly except when I would remember how long I had been away from my wife and daughter, Lisa. Fuyo and I wrote each other often, but that is not substitute for the real thing.

When it came time to get my orders I was sure that I would get a headquarters assignment or be given a job as Director of Security and Law Enforcement somewhere. Imagine my surprise when I learned that I was going to be sent to school to become a Missile Launch Control Officer, at Ellsworth Air Force Base at Rapid City, South Dakota.

CHAPTER TWENTY:
ELLSWORTH AFB

THIS BASE IN South Dakota was to be my tenth base assignment, and one for which I was the least prepared. Of course, they were going to send me to school to learn all the technical aspects of it, but the enormity of the responsibility weighed heavily. Here, I was going to have my finger on a red button that could literally destroy millions of people. Faceless as those people might be, the duty was something that I could not consider lightly.

Home Again

It was September, 1966, when I arrived home to find that Fuyo had performed admirably in getting the move arranged and getting us packed up to go. I was concerned that our travel was to be on Labor Day, but my fears were unfounded, and the traffic was not that bad.

We stopped in Kansas to see my parents, and to let the family see Lisa, we then made our way South Dakota. There was no housing for us as yet, so we sort of existed in a motel with cooking facilities. I attended orientation and indoctrination training and took care of the various administrative tasks. We were soon on our way again to attend the major technical schools.

Technical Schools

Our first stop was Lowery Air Force Base, Illinois. It was here that I was introduced to missile systems and what made them tick. I learned how they were put together, how they worked, and how the command and control systems performed in particular.

The temporary quarters for Fuyo and I was a mouse infested motel. It was now late October and the mice were coming in from the adjacent corn fields to get out of the cold. Fuyo was like a prisoner, with a child, and in a very unfriendly environment. We now found that she was becoming ill. She was pregnant. This gave rise to repeating the old saw, "What is the second thing a military man does when he returns from overseas?" Answer: "He puts down his duffle bag."

I was not very much of a consoling husband with the studying I had to do every night to prepare for the next day's assignment. That phase was soon over and we were on our way again, like Gypsies.

Our next temporary duty was Vandenburg Air Base, California, where the missile launch training would begin. As we drove across the country with Lisa and our cat, Miiko, it was a little like our trip in 1961.

We got a furnished apartment this time, and except for Fuyo's occasional morning sickness, the pressure was a little less. We were able to spend our Christmas with friends in Los Angeles. I still remember Lisa in her cowboy hat and pajamas, dancing around on Christmas Eve.

Graduating with high marks, at the expense of spending less time with Fuyo and Lisa, we got our Gypsy gear together for the trip back to Ellsworth.

We Settle In

With another short time in a motel, we finally got base housing and moved in. The truck arrived with our household goods from storage and we started keeping house as things slowly got back to normal, that is, as normal as a Launch Officer's household can get. After paring with a Deputy Commander, we took a practice ride. I scored well enough to be sent to duty immediately. I then began the 24 hours on duty, with 48 hours off routine. It was about this time that a Commendation Medal from my Korean assignment caught up with me. I was awarded it with full honors at a parade.

Rachel

Upon settling in at our new station, Fuyo was feeling a little better. She continued to have difficulty with the pregnancy, but she was toughing it out. On Lisa's third birthday, Fuyo arranged a party for her. She did a lot of stretching and reaching, hanging balloons for decoration.

The night after the party, she complained that her back ached. On a hunch, I took her to the hospital. She was in labor. Thereafter, on March 7, 1967, Rachel Eri was born at the base hospital, weighing only three pounds, seven ounces. She was nearly three months premature.

Rachel had to be kept in an incubator for some time. Hospital care was required until she weighed enough to go home. At first there was a small hole in Rachel's heart, which frightened us to death, but as she continued to mature the hole grew shut.

We were happy with our second girl, but Fuyo had wanted to give me a boy. I certainly could not fault her contribution. The child's sex is always the man's fault.

With the naming of Rachel Eri, as with Lisa, we gave her a common first name and a Japanese middle name. Neither of the two middle names look or sound glaringly Japanese, but both are pronounced differently in Japanese than in the Jewish or Irish tongue.

Rachel could not come home from the hospital for several weeks, until she weighed at least five pounds. There was nothing I could do at home. With Fuyo home, able to take care of Lisa, and Rachel in the hospital, I signed back in from leave and went to work.

A day later, Fuyo called me in the capsule and said that she was bleeding, and that I should come home as soon as possible. I told her to call an ambulance, but she waited until I came home. The place looked like a slaughter house. I rushed her to the hospital and she was in bad shape. They gave her blood and brought her back to the living, and then they gave her a D&C operation to shut down the bleeding. After Fuyo came home, Rachel was able to come home two weeks later. The bottle and diaper routine began again.

The Capsule

I suppose a word or two about my "workplace" is in order. To go to work meant driving for many miles out to any one of several missile launch control centers. Each center controlled ten silos of missiles. The center was located within a huge concrete egg, buried from 60 to 90 feet underground, depending upon the density of the soil.

The control center was manned by only two men, a commander and his deputy. They were on duty twenty-four hours or longer until relieved. Access to the control center was through a huge, seven ton blast door, which had to be opened with a hand operated hydraulic pump. The door was seldom opened except for crew changes and delivery of meals.

Meals were prepared by a support staff stationed at the surface. They would call us to ensure that nothing of importance was going on, and then they would bring our meals down in the elevator.

The staff also maintained, and frequently tested, the big generator at the surface. It powered our small motor generator. If we lost surface power our batteries in the "egg" would keep us operational for some time ... time enough to launch. The support staff on the surface was not protected in any way by a hardened (bomb proof) site. I suppose they thought them expendable.

The center was suspended within the "egg" on big shock absorbers about three feet in diameter. Under the floor of the center was a motor generator set that ran constantly converting alternating current to direct current. We had several types of communications located in the capsule: Ultra low frequency radio, high frequency radio, single sideband, broadcast, and the Strategic Air Command emergency notification system.

We wore side arms at all times, not so much to shoot your partner if he should run amok, but to force him to turn the key if the order came to do so. It was a two man operation. Both men had to agree and turn the keys at the same time. The keys were kept locked up and we took them out only if the order came, or to inventory them at shift change time. Otherwise our combination locks were both securing the safe.

When the roads were bad or time was a problem, we were sent to the command centers by helicopter. One helicopter would deliver three to four crews at a time. There were times when the weather would ground the choppers as well, and we would have to stay on duty for more than one shift. My maximum stay was three days below at one time. Others had been forced to stay as much as four days. That does not mean we were both awake. One of us could sleep, while the other would monitor communications, but you had to be prepared to act in a moment's notice. It should be noted that there were no showers. The only amenity was a chemical toilet.

If there was an emergency and we lost contact with the outside world and our support from top side, the only way out was to knock the lugs off an escape hatch. The sand was "supposed" to drain out and you could climb up the slanting pipe to the surface. There, at some undisclosed point, you were "supposed" to be able to break through the top soil. Everyone always joked that the escape hatch exited under a paved parking lot with a truck over it. No one ever had to test that theory.

Wearing the Black Hat

Due to my performance, I was promoted to "Standboard" crew. This was short for Standardization Board. With my deputy, I was to administer "check rides," or hands-on tests of other crews' missile launch capability. Our symbol of authority was to wear a black hat and a black scarf. We no longer had to drive to a missile site, but were able to fly in a helicopter to any site in need of a test.

My deputy and I now only occasionally pulled a tour of duty to maintain our own proficiency. This gave me a little more time at home which I quickly burned up studying for my degree.

The Graduate Degree

The Air Force Institute of Technology made arrangements to offer a graduate degree in Economics with a minor in Management at the base for those missile officers interested in volunteering. I felt it would help my career, what there was left of it. I was still hoping to make regular Air Force so that I could be promoted to Lieutenant Colonel before I retired.

The degree would be from South Dakota State University. They sent professors to an old Army anti-aircraft installation near the base. They equipped it with a good library and hired first rate instructors for the courses.

The long hours in the capsule were now taken up with studying for my degree. The program was not all that difficult until it came to writing the thesis, which was very time consuming with all of the research required. I really deserted the family while I was studying for my degree. The word came that I was not to be regular Air Force and that I would have to retire at the end of my 20 years. It was nip and tuck whether I could finish my course work before I retired.

Time-wise, I barely made it. I graduated *magna cum laude*.

We Wind Down Military Life

It was time to start thinking about what I was going to do in civilian life. A lot of the men in my shoes were taking advantage of the graduate degree and were going to colleges to teach. I didn't much care for the life of a teacher, so I decided I should look elsewhere and use my undergraduate degree to become a City Manager.

In the meantime, I arranged for the military to send me to a couple of hospitals to evaluate me for a medical discharge. I was still bothered by asthma, and had developed painful arthritis. This would delay my original date set, and could result in a possible percentage of a medical disability discharge. I spent a week's TDY being evaluated, then not satisfied with the results, I asked for a reevaluation at another hospital. I went to Brooks Army Hospital in Texas to appeal the first finding. In the final analysis I was granted a 40% disability. To justify that they did in fact do something, the review board lowered one factor 5% and raised another factor 5%, so the original percentage of disability remained the same.

After receiving a firm separation date from the Air Force, I began generating a comprehensive resume. Most of my peers, who were retiring around the same time that I was, were looking to colleges and universities, and "9 for 9." This meant nine months of work (teaching) for $9,000. The thought of being a teacher did not appeal to me that much, and in addition, any jobs that would whet my interest would have to pay more than that. I was looking for something in the area of public administration, which would use more of the skills that I had acquired during my military career. This was in addition to the training in my undergraduate college major.

As part of my searching, I took various Federal Civil Service tests. To my disappointment, I found that passing the tests and being qualified for high level positions did not get one a job. I felt sure that my degree in public administration could be parlayed into something lucrative, so I concentrated my efforts in that area. I joined the City Management Association, and used their position announcements to plaster the nation with applications. I had not received many favorable responses, and my time in the service was growing very short.

My search for a job as a City Manager led to an interview in Slater, Missouri. It was a very small town, about 90 miles east of Kansas City. Slater did not appear on any but the most detailed of Missouri State maps. When I flew to Kansas City, even the car rental agency had to find a state road map to guide me to the town. Their regular area maps were of no use. My first impression of Slater was that it was a small, rustic community with few prospects of growth. It was unfortunate that that was still my impression when I left over two years later.

However, I figured that I could spend some time here then move on. At least I could gain some experience in the interim. They could not afford to pay much, but I took the job. I was surprised that they offered it to me since I had absolutely no experience in the field, but I did come cheap.

The day finally came when the commander invited me into his office, gave me a medal, shook my hand and said, "Thanks a lot." That was officially the end of my military career. We called the movers to pack us up and we were on our way to Slater, Missouri.

The next part of my little saga begins with my life as a civilian again, and starting a new profession with my family. This part is entitled Part V, "The Cold Cruel World."

PART V:
THE COLD CRUEL WORLD

CHAPTER TWENTY-ONE:
SLATER, MISSOURI

THE CITY OFFICIALS were very friendly and were impressed with my age and life experience more than anything else. They had become disenchanted with young men fresh from college, who had a lot of new (and expensive) ideas, and who were not really in sync with the less sophisticated persons of the community. Drawing upon my own rural background, I was able to convince everyone that I could understand their point of view and do the job for them.

It was easy to see that they were not in a position to pay very much in the way of a salary. This was the reason that they had been forced to hire young inexperienced persons in the past. Since I was retired, we could live comfortably upon my retirement and the salary that Slater would pay. Of greater importance was the fact that I could get considerable experience, and not feel embarrassed by quitting after a couple of years to move on to a larger community.

In career terms, for the same or greater salary, I could have taken a lower ranking position, such as an assistant city manager in a large city. My age had much to do with the decision. I did not feel that I had the time to work my way up the career ladder. I did feel, however, that I would be able to move laterally in less time to reach the top level of my "incompetence." It was a case of being the "Big frog in a small pond, or a small frog a big pond". I never regretted the decision I made. However, I'm not sure that Fuyo completely understood my reasons for putting her and the children in this somewhat out of the way community. It had no theater, no white linen restaurant, and little or no social activity except for church and school. There certainly were no Japanese in the community.

I recall one incident that served to keep me from getting too big for my britches. There were some residences in Slater that were still using outdoor toilets, even though they were on the sewage system. One of my tasks included convincing an older lady that she had to abandon her "two-holer." I knew that her son held a well-paying position in another city, and I suggested to her that her son could help her out in order to install an indoor bathroom. She said, "Perhaps he could, he works for a living. It isn't as if he had a city job." Although I continued to work for some level of government from then on, I never forgot her deprecating remark.

When I felt that I had rendered Slater a service, and that I was ready to move, I began to blanket the country again with a résumé. It now looked better with a couple of years' experience reflected, and membership in the International City Management Association listed as an organization.

I continued to stay alert for another position so that by the time I had spent an appropriate period of time with the city, I could move on with a clear conscience. One response to my several queries came with a visit from the Mayor of Highland, Illinois. He was looking for another manager since the city had just fired one. He wanted to see me and speak with me before inviting me for a formal interview.

I did not hear from Highland for several months. When I did, I found that the Mayor who had visited me had been beaten in an election and there was to be a referendum eliminating the position of City Manager. The new Mayor asked if I was willing to take the job at the risk of having the position eliminated. I told him I would take the risk, and would make my pitch to the voters. The main reason I considered the job was the big difference in salary. It was much more than the small town of Slater could afford to pay.

CHAPTER TWENTY-TWO:
HIGHLAND, ILLINOIS

I **MOVED TO** Highland and left Fuyo, Lisa and Rachel behind for a month or two while I not only electioneered to hold the job, but looked for housing at the same time.

Highland, which was on the periphery of the Greater St. Louis Metropolitan Statistical Area, had a great potential for growth. I thought that if things went well I could grow with it. Since it was nearly three times the size of Slater, and since I saw considerable potential, I was willing to make the move, even in the face of the threatened referendum to eliminate the City Manager form of government.

This community had several amenities that we had not had in Slater. It had a movie theater, several restaurants, a hospital, golf course, country club and several social clubs. We were also within a short drive of St. Louis and the amenities that it had to offer.

I made the rounds of the community, gave a lot of speeches, and joined a few business clubs such as the Rotary, Optimists, The Chamber of Commerce, and the like. It was in these clubs that the real movers and shakers of the community were members. I used every possible opportunity to push for the City Manager form. The referendum to eliminate the position failed, and I was to remain as manager.

Three major functions seemed to pervade my activities during my tenure in Highland. These were: trying to keep the electrical plant in operation, building a waste water disposal plant and building our own house.

When we first arrived there was not much in the way of housing to be had, and Fuyo made several trips back and forth to Slater, until we could find some decent quarters. Our last choice seemed to be a rental. So rent we did, but what we ended up renting was a "chicken coop." In actuality it was a remodeled brooder house, in which the chickens were raised to fryer or layer stage. It had been plumbed and paneled, and a few other touches added to turn it into a halfway livable place for the family to be together. One reason for that decision was that the "chicken coop" was owned and rented by one of the city councilmen.

While in our chicken coop we were desperately looking for a place to live. As an older community, Highland's housing stock was very old and limited. There were three new subdivisions being built, but all of the houses were pre-sold.

Then the opportunity to purchase a vacant lot arose. It was in a good location, so we decided to hire an architect and a contractor and build our own house. We added our own ideas to the architect's and we were soon under construction.

The builder moved along very quickly and we were under roof in surprisingly good time. The slowest thing was our indecision as to what fixtures, appliances, colors, floor coverings, and the like that we wanted. We hadn't realized all the decisions that we would have to make.

Our design called for huge exposed timbers, with a long, gently sloping roof, and solid redwood planking for the vertical siding. The house was beautiful, and we looked forward to the redwood turning to its natural patina. Imagine our sinking feeling when we passed by years later to find that the new owners had covered that beautiful redwood planking with aluminum siding.

However, nothing lasts forever. After about three years, the political climate changed, and a new regime ran on a ticket of eliminating the City Manager position again as a cost saving action. The feeling was that the board could do all that I was doing.

Thus, I was soon cast adrift and I began papering the world with my résumé. I was not too long unemployed, and found a nice little community of Napoleon, Ohio that would have me.

CHAPTER TWENTY-THREE:
NAPOLEON, OHIO

NAPOLEON WAS A prosperous little community of about ten thousand population, located on the Maumee River south of Toledo. The economy was agri-business. Most of the vegetable crops grown locally went into the making of Campbell Soup. That company had a big plant in Napoleon. In fact, one of their Vice Presidents had been elected to the City Council. Napoleon had a strong sense of community with a lot of spirit and camaraderie.

The Job

The big capital projects for me here were to establish an industrial park and to construct a high voltage electrical transmission line around the city to serve industry and the growing population. The previous person in the position had been an electrical engineer, holding the high paying title of Director of Utilities. He also performed basic administration tasks for the city. I was to do the same job at nearly half the salary of the engineer. My title would be City Manager. Though I thought the inequity stunk, I was not in a very good position to quibble. I had been a few months without a job, and this position looked very much to my liking. In addition, the salary was a bit better than in Highland, even if it was less than that of the engineer.

My first cross with the City Fathers came when I came back to Highland for Thanksgiving with my family. The river bar screens for the water plant had failed, then a pump failed and Napoleon was without water. They called me at home and seemed disappointed that I did not immediately return to help dig the dead fish out of the clogged pipes. There was little I could do, but I headed back to Napoleon after finishing dinner.

Life Without the Family

It was pretty rough batching it without the family. The first task of survival was finding an apartment of some sort. There seemed to be nothing satisfactory right in town, so I ended up in a small room in a little community south of town. The room was acceptable, but the apartment complex was on wells instead of city water and the high sulphur and iron content of the water put a thick black scale on the sink and bath tub, and the water was undrinkable it smelled so bad. I stayed there for a month until I could find an apartment in town. I knew that if Fuyo, Lisa and Rachel ever visited, I could not possibly have room for them there at the old place.

The new apartment was nice. It had city water and cable. It was fully furnished and I needed little more than sheets and pillow cases. It was here that I stayed the rest of my months in Napoleon.

Most of my off-duty hours were spent in the office or at the Elks Club. It was a home away from home, with nightly bridge games and interesting conversation. Some of our bridge games adjourned to private residences where we would play until three or four in the morning. We would then go out to breakfast at the truck stop. I would get home in time to change and go to work. On several occasions I would drive to Highland on the weekend, but was always afraid something more would happen while I was gone that would require my attention.

Fuyo, Lisa and Rachel came to visit me once. We went house hunting. For some reason there did not seem to be a very good assortment of available houses for us. We had probably been spoiled by our big house in Highland. We looked at dozens. I had already scratched some of the smaller, and the not so respectable looking houses, from the list of those available. I knew that Fuyo would certainly not want to look at those.

I Start Looking Again

There was any number of things that caused me to place my name into the pot again for another position. There seemed to be no house that satisfied us in Napoleon, and we certainly did not wish to build another one, at least not right away. The city was not paying me the salary that the last person had drawn, though I had much the same responsibilities. Only because this person had the title of Engineer, did they feel that they could pay me less. Lastly, the commute was a long way, and since we had not yet sold the house in Highland, I thought perhaps that I could get back to Illinois, even though I had applied to other places as well.

One of my many applications had generated some interest in Westmont, Illinois. Without any notice to me, the mayor and one trustee of that community came to Napoleon and walked about the business district asking questions about me. The banker, the real estate people, and several business people were asked how I was doing and what kind of a manager I was. The local newspaper later ran a column suggesting that the Chicago Mafia was trying to kidnap me. The Village of Westmont then invited me for an interview. After one of the toughest grillings yet, I beat out four other candidates. They offered me the job. One of the most thrilled was Fuyo. She had not wanted to take yet another state driver's license test.

CHAPTER TWENTY-FOUR:
WESTMONT, ILLINOIS

WESTMONT WAS A Village of about twelve thousand people located in the western suburbs of Chicago, about 20 miles from the Loop. It is almost totally surrounded by other suburbs similar to it.

The job here entailed a greater variety of administrative skills, primarily finance and industrial development. The problem was to control growth rather than to indiscriminately welcome it as I did in Napoleon.

There was a large staff, and resources that I could finally bring to bear on the city's problems. Regarding the family, there was a good school for the children, the proximity of Japanese food stores for Fuyo, and recreation, social opportunities not available with previous jobs.

Spending longer here than at any other job, we were becoming pretty much grounded in this community, but as often happens with City Manager positions, politics reared its ugly head.

Transition

After I resigned from my position as City Manager, I took an early retirement from the Illinois Municipal Retirement System. I then began to put out a few feelers through the City Management Association for a new place to light.

Since I had retired from the Illinois system and was drawing a monthly check, I would have to go out of state for my next management job or give up my retirement. My family did not want to move again. The girls were in high school and Fuyo had friends she didn't want to lose. With that in mind, I began to look about for a source of revenue.

My early retirement from the Municipal Retirement System had a provision for accelerated payout until Social Security kicked in. We were able to get by, but not in the manner in which we would like to become accustomed. I was still keeping my eyes open for ways to have less macaroni and cheese for breakfast, lunch and dinner.

To keep my hand in, I prepared a letterhead with "Bishop's Consulting Services" in bold letters, and had a few business cards printed. I was a Certified Planner so I could do land use consulting. I was already helping the people in a local assisted housing facility with their administration. I had studied the HUD regulations, took a day-long course and a day-long test and became a Certified Assisted Housing Consultant.

For all my preparation I obtained only one land use consulting client, but I did get a lot of billable hours with the housing project. It is amazing how much you can charge per hour when you are a "consultant" and have a pretty gold-sealed certificate to that effect.

A friend suggested that I join her in an insurance sales program that worked very much like a pyramid scheme. You sold a policy to a friend or two, and those friends were each to sell to their friends, and so on. I would collect a commission for each policy I sold, plus I would get a commission for the policies sold by those to whom I had initially sold, all the way up the pyramid.

I went to several classes, studied for a broker's license, took all the tests, obtained a broker's license, and received my insurance license. Then, after all the excitement of the classes and the tests, and the meetings and briefings, I said to myself, "I am **not** an insurance salesman."

In careful introspection, I decided that the idea left me cold. I did not sell one policy. I did, however, keep my licenses current for a couple of years "just in case." This was much like what I had done with my steam engineer's license that I qualified for in the State of Ohio. Needless to say there were no commissions from that venture.

While I was lazing away on this lacuna, I thought this would be a good time to add a few more accounting and tax preparation classes in readiness for sitting for the CPA examination. Over the years, the requirements for the license kept becoming more stringent. I always seemed to be playing catch-up. I had been doing accounting and tax returns for many years, and was confident that I could pass the test, but I needed certain accredited hours of classroom time. I enrolled in the College of DuPage and went to night school between the times I was attending the insurance sales course.

One day, out of the blue, a city manager friend from another community called me about a potential job opening with the State of

Illinois. He said that he had been offered the job, but he had just taken his retirement and wanted to enjoy it. I told him I was interested, so he gave me the name and number of the contact person.

I had been vaguely aware of The Department of Commerce and Community Affairs (DCCA, pronounced "dekka" for short). It provided several kinds of assistance to municipalities, townships, counties and special districts. It also operated the State Film Office and the state's version of a Better Business Bureau. The big thrust was economic development.

I called my friend's contact to inquire about the job. He asked me a few questions and invited me to Chicago for an interview. They were starting a new project and were looking for persons with financial and municipal experience to work in the Department of Commerce and Community Affairs.

The interview in Chicago was with an assistant director and a bureau chief. The reason that my friend had been called was that they were looking for someone with city management skills. The goal was for the State to assist small municipalities with their administration, accounting and financial matters in a hands-on capacity.

The job sounded interesting, and "up my alley," so I agreed to sign on with them after they ran my name through their personnel system and formally offered me the job. I thought to myself, "Oh boy, don't mess this up, I smell a sinecure here."

CHAPTER TWENTY-FIVE:
DCCA

THE JOB WITH DCCA required a daily commute to Chicago, which was certainly something new to me. Fuyo would drive me to the station and I would take the train. On occasion I would take a State car home when I was to drive to an outlying community the next day. This meant a two way commute by auto. This pretty much confirmed that if I had to commute by automobile on a daily basis--I wouldn't!

As a Revenue and Fiscal Advisor for the State of Illinois, I had duties much like that of a City Manager, but without the many responsibilities for the Police Department, Fire Department and Public Works. Instead of one city I might have several at the same time. I did analyses for municipal finances, and municipal utilities, assisted smaller communities with their budgets, their tax ordinances and water and sewer rate studies.

I had two other "advisors" under me and we were responsible for those municipalities in the northern half of the state which requested our services. The southern half of the state was serviced by three advisors based in Springfield, the capitol. Often we were required to drive to Springfield for an office conference. We would compare notes, get new assignments, pick up new printed materials, and the like. It required an overnight in Springfield, but we were compensated for the expense.

It was on this job that I was forced to learn hands-on use of computers for the first time. Not only did I learn to use spread sheets and data processing, but I was first introduced to the simple task of word processing. Heretofore, the typewriter and adding machine were the limit of my office machine skills. Of course, the municipalities where I was manager had used automated billing and accounting, but I had not learned how to actually operate any of the systems.

Since the position was rather political and most fellow employees owed their position to knowing someone in politics, I became rather steeped in the world of political favoritism. Since I had obtained my job without any political influence, I was surprised to learn how many owed their job to an elected official.

Running for Public Office

Back in Westmont, without any campaigning for the job at all, but after a check with me that I would accept the job, I was appointed as a Precinct Committeeman. I took that job seriously, and soon, on evenings and weekends, I was going door to door with a little monthly newsletter I had prepared for the precinct. Not long after that, I was visited at home by some party representatives with a request that I announce for the position of County Board member for my district. I soon learned that there was more than one faction of the party, and that I would have opposition. I discussed the situation with Fuyo and we weighed the problems and difficulties.

Counting upon my recognition as a previous City Manager and my work in the neighborhoods, I decided to give it a try. My first hurdle was to obtain approval from the State to allow an employee to run for public office in a County. There were cautions about conflict of interest, but approval was granted.

The next hurdle was fund raising. I was lucky to do well, but there was a need for some infusion of my own money. It was not that much of a strain on my own pocket book, but I really hated going to people, hat-in-hand, asking for money. I felt like a beggar. Right away I knew I didn't have the right stuff for political office.

I received good feedback from a TV interview spot, and I seemed to be doing well at the various speaking engagements. In addition, I had several good endorsements, but it wasn't enough. To cut to the chase, I was beaten rather soundly. The defeat was not good for my ego at all, but I didn't let it bother me.

With that, I quit politics for good. Fuyo, was certainly not unhappy about that. She was fed up with walking from door to door with campaign literature, and I was tired of shaking hands with people I did not much care for. I guess I was sort of relieved that I lost. I didn't want to keep having all that campaign hassle at regular intervals.

So, it was back to my advisor job with no distractions. I wrote several manuals on finance for use by municipalities, and the job stayed interesting. I enjoyed the work a lot, but all good things must come to an end. I had purchased additional years retirement service by use of military service and service as a municipal manager in other states. This placed me in a pretty comfortable retirement bracket.

We Build Again

Not yet retired but on the verge of doing so, we decided to build a new house and move. I believe that if women could remember the pain and agony of childbirth, there might be fewer children born. So too it was with building a custom home. There is the agony of the hundreds of decisions to be made with which you must live later. For example: the finding a proper lot for your envisioned home, the selection of the builder and the architect, then there is the selection of electrical fixtures, appliances, tile, color schemes, brick, cabinetry, landscaping ... the list goes on. We had forgotten what we had to go through for our first custom home, but it was worth it.

We moved in, had an open house party, and faced all the questions of, "what do you empty nesters need with such a big house?" My answer was always, "It gives me more places to hide from my wife."

The house turned out very nice. It was unique, modern, and quite livable. My favorite place was the room we dubbed the library, but it was part den and part office as well. After a session of typing this very document, I could grab a book and flop down on the couch to recharge my think tank. I have more books than I can ever read. For years I have been collecting books, and each time I would buy one I would say, "I'll read this when I retire." Well, if I should start now, and do nothing but read, eat and sleep, I would probably make only a small dent before they carried me off.

CHAPTER TWENTY-SIX:
RETIREMENT

FUYO AND I were planning a trip to Japan for a wedding in her family and we were combining that with a long tour of China. I used up my accrued vacation time for the trip then put in my application for retirement.

In the meantime, I was now over 65 and drawing Social Security. In fact, a few of my checks were cut back because I was still on the clock with the State. Now, with military retirement, the municipal retirement, the Social Security, and the State Employee's Retirement, I figured that we wouldn't have to pick up soda cans along the road.

I became a little more conservative with my investments. I had two brokers and both of them "cried the blues" that I was no longer trading as much. The only hitch was living long enough to enjoy it. We were now able to spend much more time enjoying our grandchildren.

To catch up on our family, chronologically, Lisa had joined the Army after graduating from nursing school at Northwestern. She found a doctor while in the service and we had a wonderful wedding for them in San Antonio, at an historic church near the Alamo. They gave us four lovely grandchildren. Ben recently retired from the Army as a full colonel and will continue to practice medicine.

Rachel graduated with a degree in Journalism from Creighton University. While there, she dated a boy she knew from our home town who was pursuing his Pharmacy degree. They were engaged, and we gave them a nice wedding here at home. Rachel and Eugene soon gave us three beautiful granddaughters.

Our children married well, and it gives one a sense of closure to know that they are happy, well-adjusted and carrying on our genes.

After we both retired, Fuyo and I travelled a lot. We toured some 42 countries. I took lots of pictures and I faithfully kept a journal of all our tours. We hardly ever look at the pictures or the journals now, however. Travelling was a lot of fun, but as we got older some of the tours were a bit strenuous, and we were getting a bit creaky.

I cast about for something to occupy my time. I certainly didn't want to vegetate. Fuyo and I couldn't travel all the time. That gets old after a while. Our yard would not accommodate much gardening, and I kept telling myself that digging in the dirt was too much like farming. I had had my fill of that many years before.

We soon became interested in stained glass. We took a course, and bought a lot of equipment: diamond saws, grinders, soldering irons, antiquing chemicals, etc. Our enthusiasm lasted through about three major projects before we lost interest. My last project was constructing six stained glass inserts for the clerestory windows of our great room and dining room.

It is a very exacting hobby, and I sometimes became very frustrated that a sliver of glass would not fit. Glass is very unforgiving, so it always meant cutting a new piece. I was not so upset when a piece broke when cutting. This was to be expected on occasion, but a piece the fraction of an inch too large or too small was cause for self-flagellation.

Fuyo had her sewing projects, reading, and her bridge with many clubs and groups, so she did not suggest any more joint hobbies. I then figured that I would write a science fiction novel. After all, I had started an SF story when I was in the third or fourth grade. I would find it, flesh it out a bit and finish it.

Whoa there! I read my first draft. It was so funny that I was in stitches. It wasn't meant to be funny, but when Arvalla made moon eyes at Dirk, the rocket pilot, I knew it was time to crank up the shredder. Science Fiction is not as hackneyed as it had been in the past, so careful thought must be given to subject matter. Technology is outrunning fiction. Then, of course, there is the possibility of infringement upon another author's work. It seemed as if I would have to read everything to make sure the plot had not been done before. Then there were subjects that were either taboo or politically incorrect to be allowed in a marketable novel.

As a writer, I somehow questioned mainstream ideas. I wanted to make a statement of some sort, no matter how small or ineffective. A novel, I thought, that dealt with non-mainstream ideas might be a possible endeavor. What was the most common of that genre? Why, erotica of course.

I started anew, and struggled mightily with deciding upon an exact plot, and setting out a cast of characters, I then began my writing. As is often case with neophytes like myself, my ambition exceeded my endeavor. I expected to have a novel finished in short order, but that was not to be.

Once I had the story put together, I could not leave it alone. I would pit it, pat it, massage it, change it, and toy with it until I wore out both the story and myself. I would then shelve the whole thing and start over from scratch with another plot and cast of characters. I figured that if I couldn't satisfy myself, how could I interest readers? I slowly let myself get out of the mood of writing a novel or anything else, but then, to satisfy my itch, I produced this.

Thanks for reading.

O. R. Bishop
2012

ABOUT THE AUTHOR

I have an undergraduate degree in Public Administration (cum laude), a graduate degree in Economics (magna cum laude). I have many years of administrative positions to include City Manager, State Revenue and Fiscal Advisor, commissioned officer in the military, and as a consultant in land use planning, and assisted housing.

I have always been comfortable about writing from the time I was in grade school when I wrote Science Fiction. I wrote several financial administration manuals while in State government and have continued to write short stories for my own amusement after I retired.

My wife and I now live in a suburb of Chicago where we retired, and maintain an active life of travel and social bridge, as well as reading and surfing the 'Net.'

Oliver R. Bishop